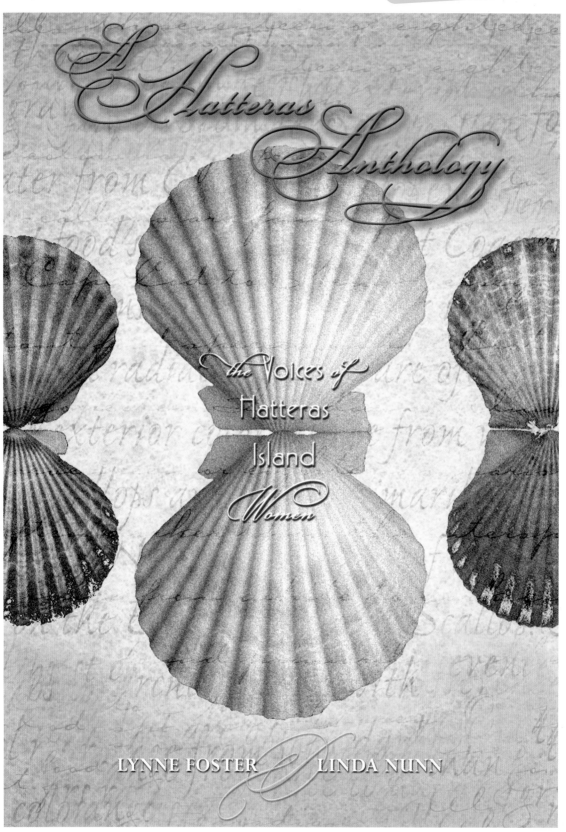

A Hatteras Anthology

the Voices of Hatteras Island Women

LYNNE FOSTER & LINDA NUNN

[Outer Banks Press]

A Hatteras Anthology
The Voices of Hatteras Island Women
Lynne Hoffman Foster and Linda Elizabeth Nunn

An Outer Banks Press Book
Published in 2003 by Outer Banks Press, a subsidiary of OBBC, Inc.

ISBN 0-9713890-3-9

Library of Congress Cataloging-in-Publication data available by request.

Editors: Lynne Hoffman Foster and Linda Elizabeth Nunn
Cover Design and Book Design: Linda L. Lauby, Outer Banks Press
Cover Image and Interior Botanical Images: Jeff Venier, Getty Images

Second Printing

Printed in China

For bulk purchases, special sales and book signings, please contact:

Outer Banks Press
Post Office Box 2829
Kitty Hawk, North Carolina 27949
252.261.0612
252.261.0613 FAX
mail@outerbankspress.com
WWW.OUTERBANKSPRESS.COM

Outer Banks Press is an independent publisher specializing in fine magazines and books of literary and photographic merit, distinctive in both content and design.

A Hatteras Anthology

Enjoy our voices!
Lynne

the Voices of

Hatteras

Island

Women

LYNNE HOFFMAN FOSTER   LINDA ELIZABETH NUNN

TABLE OF CONTENTS

ACKNOWLEDGMENTS

The best adventures are usually undertaken with friends. We offer our sincere gratitude to the following for their support and encouragement:

To Irene Nolan, editor, Barbara Satterthwaite and Donna Barnett at *The Island Breeze*;

To Helen Mills Wilson, information advocate;

To Linda Marie Turner and Brenda Johnson, reading committee;

To the memory of Priscilla Hine DeLong, jubilant artist;

To Georgia Hardee, owner, To The Point Publishing;

To Mary Helen Goodloe-Murphy, journalist, *The Coastland Times*;

To Cornelia Poe Olive, editor, *The Outer Banks Sentinel*;

And to the many women who contributed their work, their time and their energy, we thank you for your voice, for "speaking from your hearts."

INTRODUCTION

There are still places left in this country where people move to the rhythms of the seasons and geography is more than a classroom subject; where the Weather Channel isn't gospel, and experience and senses are; where the season and the weather determine if you work on any given day and, if you do, what work you perform. Where many people have enough and would rather enjoy their world than work in it too much. Summers are full – full of work, full of tourists, full of traffic. Winters are quiet. Winters are for surfing or fishing in Mexico and Costa Rica and for all those books that want to be read all summer when eight hours of much-needed sleep require a 9 p.m. bedtime, despite music blaring from visiting pick-up trucks. More important, oyster roasts and pig-pickins, covered-dish suppers and community meetings provide our chance to strengthen bonds of friendship and support, as do traditional Southern "visits." Winter is our time to have our home to ourselves.

Here on Hatteras Island, North Carolina, our slender barrier island, the effects of nature's forces are immediate. We stand witness to the magnificence of Mother Nature's follies and furies. As the shoreline shifts, so do our moods. As the seasons change, so do our very lives. A sound, or lack thereof, the dry or moist sensations on our skin, a stillness or frenzy in the air, the strength of the sea smell: all toll warnings we had better heed. Our eyes adjust to the unfamiliar and even to that which is not beautiful. Where once stood a maritime forest, are now very, very tall sticks – but a few dogwood blossoms grow beneath the dim canopy. A beach gets thinner and then it gets wider. A shipwreck appears and then it disappears. Dunes are sand hills, and then sand flats. There are days when you feel you could walk across Oregon Inlet and there are days when you are wading through your own yard and little boys are catching fish in the streets. Our only bridge is frail; our single road is even more so. Some years you can't give crabs away; some years you pay nearly thirty dollars for a picked pound. Fish are here and then they are not and then they are back again. Businesses come and businesses go. Often they go quickly – like the fragile land mass on which we live.

Every summer (and spring and fall too as seasons expand) we are bombarded with questions about our lives and with expressions of longing for what many believe to be our lives. Regardless of age or experience, many of our visitors believe that if they just lived on the island too, they could enjoy paradise, where no one has to really work. There is no cancer, no drugs, no money worries, no accidents, no violence or pain; not even death reaches us.

They are vacationing, and they ask why things cost so much. They don't, really, when compared to the world's other Edens. Motels, restaurants and so-called "cottages" are less expensive than they are at other coastal resorts. Living here does cost though. We have one of the highest costs of living in the state and yet our income levels rank among the lowest.

The costs are more than monetary. So are the benefits. Convenience is something we don't enjoy – and many of us don't want to. We support small local businesses. Our friends and neighbors own them and they have proven to be available to us even in the worst conditions. If we have to evacuate the island and the banks are closed, cash is ready; if a storm comes and goes and comes back and hangs around, there is drinking water and other necessities; if our bodies are damaged our doctor is here and can get to us somehow – he has waders too. Something serious may require a helicopter to carry the patient off island. Dare County provides the ride unless the weather warrants the larger and heavier Coast Guard chopper; sometimes even that can't make it. We all know when someone has been taken off the island because the landing and take-off are cause for the fire siren to blare and the volunteers to race to support the flight. If our homes or businesses are damaged, the local hardware store will open its doors and neighbors will help with the labor. For most of the islanders this support is worth far more than dollars.

It is an island tradition that the women hold the families and communities together. This is no doubt true elsewhere, but in such a macho environment it is exaggerated. Many women thrive here and find a persona they didn't know existed. They support one another and they enjoy their lives, reveling not only in extraordinary friendships and rich marriages and partnerships, but also in nature's extremes. Yet, some don't. For them, there are limited resources. It is never easy to ask for help, especially when you feel so "exposed" and when there are few choices. Outer Banks Hotline grows at an alarming pace, doing an amazing outreach. But they can only help those who come to them for their help and many women wait until their situation is dire – if they come at all. Our girls, too, often lack the confidence needed to do well. Too many go off to college only to last one year and return to the island unprepared to do much more than clean massive rental cottages, de-head shrimp in one of the local restaurants, or stand for long hours in yet another T-shirt emporium, where they await the end of the tourist season and their subsequent unemployment checks.

It takes worldly experience and maturity to truly appreciate life on a barrier island. It is a good place to be when you are somewhat world-weary, very curious or simply sensual. It is not a good place when your dreams exceed your possibilities and when you long for more. That applies equally to the young native and to the older newcomer who gets here and finds she misses what she had from back wherever she came. However, more and more young women go off the island to college each fall and choose to return to the island to take on leadership roles and practice new skills, enriching their home villages and the entire island. There is also a growing population of "newcomers" who have embraced life here, and their contributions are invaluable as they volunteer their talents and time and teach us all to better appreciate our natural gifts.

There are numerous silent voices here. We approached many women and asked for their stories and their thoughts, their creativity and insights. Some responded, and of course, some did not. Those who did have eloquently related various aspects of their experiences on Hatteras Island through their words, their music, and their creative eyes and hands, honoring all of the Hatteras Island women. Their works have moved us and we are pleased to share them with you.

Lynne Hoffman Foster
September 14, 2002
Hatteras Island, North Carolina

INTRODUCTION

A satellite view of our island shows a thin, gently curving line of green mimicking the coast of North Carolina, as if an emerald thread raveled from the warp of the mainland fabric and drifted away. This view is always startling to many of us who make a life here – we wonder just what it is we are doing thirty miles out to sea, on a fragile strip of sand that bellies up to the turbulent convergence of the Labrador Current and the Gulf Stream.

Here, furious storms regularly alter our geography, change the landscape of our villages, change the patterns of our lives. Here, we learn to live in tandem with nature, to accommodate our lifestyles to the singular identity of a barrier island, to deal with issues uncommon to many other locales and habitats. We adjust and adapt to an often tenuous existence because the rewards are many. We live hand in hand with a precarious beauty, alongside abundant wildlife, under a splendid sky, beside the ever constant, life-sustaining, life-stealing sea.

Those who are born here come from stoic and resilient men and women of pliant determination and quiet courage. Their heritage is one of endurance and consistent rapport with the sea. Tempted by the allure of island life, those who come to stay rapidly learn the reality – that jubilance is tempered by jeopardy. It is said that Hatteras Island men and women are a class unto themselves. It is our belief that the women shine the brighter.

When the idea for this book came about, we met at Lynne's kitchen table (where else?) and began to plan our project. Our daily lives place us in contact with the public, and talking to other women is as natural and necessary as sunshine on our upturned faces. Beneath the customary chatter about the ordinary and the routine, we heard the reasonable whispers of quiet dreams and altered ambitions. If you talk to a woman long enough, and listen with an honest ear, you will hear her speaking from her heart. We wanted to turn up the volume on those whispers and heart sounds, and we conceived this anthology as a way to give a clearly audible voice to our island sisters.

We began to sort through our ideas, to raise questions and find answers. As our excitement grew, we shared our ideas with a few other women, then a few more, until we had a merry band of enthusiastic and supportive women sharing the abundant possibilities of our adventure. The project blossomed as woman after woman welcomed the opportunity to say what was on her mind, to share her concerns and her talent, to validate her life as a barrier island woman. We believe that, like a seashell dropped into a tidal pool, the happy consequences of our endeavors will spread through ever-widening circles, born of the voices of these Hatteras Island women.

Linda Elizabeth Nunn
September 14, 2002
Hatteras Island, North Carolina

Melanie Schwarzer

Melanie Schwarzer grew up in Central New York. She is a former
newspaper columnist and magazine feature writer. She has been an
art dealer, ancient artifact conservator, museum registrar, accountant,
and has taught every grade from pre-school through college while
rearing two sons. During the past three decades of marriage she and
her family have moved more than two dozen times, living in many
regions of America and in Italy, Greece and Turkey. Her experiences living in small, overseas coastal villages prepared her well for
life on Hatteras Island, where she moved when her husband, Joe,
was appointed director of the Graveyard of the Atlantic Museum.

Befana in Training

Melanie Schwarzer

I grew up listening to the legend of Befana. She was the old woman with the broom who was too busy cleaning and sweeping her home to journey with the wise men who were following the star in search of the newborn baby. Of course, when she later discovered the baby was Jesus, her regret for not going was so enormous she spent the rest of eternity taking gifts to deserving children at Christmas time. In my arrogant ignorance of childhood, I could not comprehend anyone as pitifully stupid as Befana.

We knew when we moved here it would be an incredible place for stargazing. Nothing is more spectacular than a cold, clear Hatteras winter sky; the myriad stars are breathtaking and we have made good use of our telescope. My youngest son loves space, started learning to fly when he was thirteen, not far from the Kitty Hawk spot of Orville and Wilbur fame, and, in a plan that has never wavered, hopes to study aeronautics in college and eventually become an astronaut. Our family spends an inordinate amount of time watching videos about space, reading books about space, making rockets and trying to figure where we can get the material to design a wind tunnel. My husband has played the music from the film *The Earth to the Moon* so often my son has started to wear earplugs. We know every exhibit at the National Air and Space Museum in Washington by heart. Imagine our joy when we discovered that one of the unexpected perks of living on Hatteras Island was being able to view the space shuttle lift-off in Florida from our beaches. This is not something advertised in the tourist brochures, but it should be. We had heard stories about being able to observe the separation and the plumes of smoke and see the rocket speed across the sky as it passed overhead.

The lift-off for the space shuttle was scheduled for 6:11 p.m. As the time approached, we realized it was still quite light out and assumed we would probably be unable to see anything against the early evening sky. At 5:45 p.m., I put a soufflé in the oven and continued to prepare dinner. Ten minutes later, my husband and son ran into the kitchen telling me it seemed to be getting darker and they were going off to the beach to try to see the lift-off. "Come with us!" they begged. "I can't, I've got a soufflé in the oven," I moaned.

The Space Shuttle Discovery took off against a perfect Hatteras winter sunset at the appointed time. I have been told the plumes of smoke made the clouds shimmer silver. The separation arced to the heavens and the shuttle sped across the sky until it could no longer be seen when it passed the full moon.

I had missed the euphoria experienced by my husband and son on the beach. I had missed the first lift-off we would see as a family. I had missed it! Do women constantly, like Befana, miss the opportunities and moments, that are so precious, all for a dinner in the oven or sweeping a floor? Are we on Hatteras different from women anywhere? I have lived many places and there are Befanas at every turn. Befanas who are buried in minutiae, enveloped in picayune detail, grasping at a comfort zone where wrapping themselves up in committees or jobs or housework or friends keeps them from ever having to examine who they are or where they are, losing sight of the real reason they are here.

Of course, as women we all have a bit of Befana in us. Women, almost by definition, put their families or jobs or committees above themselves. I don't know if this is a maternal or societal instinct, but I sense it is a conditioned reflex from which females need to extricate themselves periodically.

Instead of the constant gifts of our time and enthusiasm for everything else, it is necessary to step away once in a while from obligations and take a different path. Women need to give them-selves an offertory of self-knowledge. How many women here, or any place, have taken the time for solitary contemplation? It is easy to do here. On this island we are bestowed with a natural scenic beauty. A walk through Buxton Woods, a stroll on the beach, a few minutes to rock on the porch make it possible to remind ourselves of our priorities.

I think most of the women who live here would choose no other place, but it is easy to become, unwittingly, a Befana clone. As for me, the next time the shuttle lifts off, we are ordering out! ☂

Trish Rucker-Dempsey

Trish Rucker-Dempsey received a degree in art from the University of Georgia at Athens. She and her husband, a hunting and fishing guide, and three sons are residents of Hatteras Village. With a variety of jobs to ensure her livelihood in "paradise," Trish teaches, and frequently works as a waitress and sales clerk. Her finely detailed sketches of island wildlife are popular with residents and visitors alike, and confirm her creativity and talent; they are available in several formats in area businesses.

Jan DeBlieu

Jan DeBlieu is the author of three books about people and nature, "Hatteras Journal" (1987), "Meant to be Wild" (1991), and "Wind" (1998). She has also written for many national magazines, including the "New York Times Magazine", "Audubon," "Smithsonian" and "Southern Living." In 1999, Wind won the John Burroughs Medal for Distinguished Natural History Writing, the nation's highest prize for natural history writers, making Jan the first woman to win the award since 1977. She lives with her husband and son on North Carolina's Outer Banks, where the landscape and culture of the islands are major components of her work.

Beauty in the Beasts
Lessons on Life in a Fish Bowl

Jan DeBlieu

In a corner of my kitchen, pushed against a wall where no ray of sunlight can reach it, is a glass container of water that holds the most intricate stirrings of life. Beneath a white washing light small animals feed and startle and feed again, as alert to danger as if they were still living in the wild waters of North Carolina's coastal sounds. As if they believed that at any time a predator could pass overhead or a change of tide could bring a sudden infusion of plankton. As if none of them – the urchin, the snapping shrimp, or the grass shrimp and burrowing worms – were encased in a glass world, dependent on a flow of electricity to keep them supplied with air.

I am what might be called an aquarium hobbyist, though friends who have seen my tank would laugh outright at that description. To keep an aquarium means assuming the role of a god: you arrange a small universe and fill it with animals whose well-being you control, or at least manipulate, from that point forth. Aquarium keeping is something like adopting a stray dog. At first, you don't realize that you're entering an immensely complex relationship, and that your life might be altered by it. You think only that it might be fun to add a few fish to the house as decorations, the way you would add a couch or a new painting. Really, how much trouble could a tank of fish be? Inevitably, you find that creating a world is not so simple – not if you want it to be as pristine and well balanced as the world outside your door.

My interest in keeping marine animals began years ago with a swarm of tiny creatures I caught by accident in a piece of drifting weed. One afternoon during a walk in the brackish marshes of Cape Hatteras, I noticed an odd, pink aquatic grass growing on a rock in Pamlico Sound. I had never seen the likes of it before. I waded out, getting soaked to my thighs, and picked a strand. I stuck it in my shirt pocket, along with several fleshy leaves from a bed of sea lettuce that grew close by.

I had just moved to Hatteras, and I wanted to learn as much as possible about the shifting world where the region's fresh rivers clasp hands with the Atlantic Ocean. Back home I stuck the limp, slimy weeds in a glass of tap water so they would fan out and be easier to identify. I glanced at the sea lettuce and flipped open a field guide to a page with fine, reddish seaweeds. A second later I looked back at the glass in astonishment. The water teemed with tiny, shrimp-like animals that had traveled home in my pocket.

It took several hours of study with a hand lens before I could identify the creatures as a species of scud, an abundant, shell-less insect with seven pairs of legs and a body as arched and flat as the top of a horseshoe. Scuds feed on the detritus that gathers on the bottoms of sounds, bays and tide pools. They are simple to keep as pets: for nine months a school of them lived in a glass container on my kitchen table, with no supplemental food, no air supply and only a couple of water changes. They grew as large as half an inch, and their eyes varied in color from muddy brown to purplish red. They moved in constant circles. The larger males swam along with females cradled beneath them, making their way industriously around the canister even as they mated. Twice I watched as a female released young from her brood pouch, curling and uncurling her body as specks of life burst out of her. Each night over dinner I studied the scuds as they bred, bore young, and consumed each other's remains.

This first, makeshift aquarium, filled with clouds of decaying matter, was in no way attractive. I lived in a small town populated mostly by island natives, and when my neighbors stopped by, they glanced at the canister as if it had become an item of local gossip. ("That new girl in Miss Ersie's place, she keeps a bottle of slimy-looking critters on her kitchen table.") Later I got a ten-gallon aquarium and stocked it with a healthy collection of scuds. They lasted only until I released a few killifish into the tank. It was the same with the fragile pink anemones and thread-like skeleton shrimp I brought home in old yogurt containers.

The delicate invertebrates that so fascinated me served as the first link in the food chain. If I wanted to keep them in the tank, I could keep nothing else.

It is interesting to look back on that period and remember my original vision for what I hope0d to create. Kept carefully, aquariums can be works of living, ever-changing art. I wanted to construct a microcosm of the estuary both to display the animals that lived there and to study them. I did feel a few pangs of guilt about taking animals captive, even something as tiny as a scud. But the idea of having my own small window into the underworld of the coastal sounds was too seductive to be ignored. In summer the clear green waters that surround Cape Hatteras fill with tropical and subtropical species, swept north by the Gulf Stream. I thought it would be a relatively simple matter to net some up.

What I did not anticipate was my own clumsiness, or how quickly I would become obsessed with obtaining beautiful creatures.

Somehow, the most exotic animals – the ornately finned blennies, colorful striped sergeants, and lithe sea horses – kept eluding my grasp. I soon grew bored with the drab gray killifish I could easily seine from a small cove near my house. They spent all their time either chasing each other or swimming in one corner of the tank, begging for food like circus animals. The dominant male had a pretty patch of neon blue on his shoulder, but within a few weeks he had nipped the tails of the smaller fish into ribbons. A friend gave me a purple urchin pried from a jetty. It traveled deftly over the sides of the tank, grazing on algae, waving its vermilion spines. A starfish I found stranded on the beach quickly learned to come to the top of the tank when I wiggled pieces of cut fish in the water; it even took pieces of fish from my hand. But these appealing animals stayed on the sidelines. The dull, pugnacious killifish dominated center stage.

I returned the killifish to the cove and went looking for replacements. I knew several people who kept aquariums stocked with locally caught fish of stunning beauty. Some, like the brightly colored wrasses and filefish, resembled living pieces of stained glass. Others were simply fun to watch, like the tiny puffer in a friend's tank that kept inflating itself into a spiky ball. I wanted creatures that were just as intriguing, and I wanted to get them by plumbing the waters around my home. Buying marine animals from a pet store, I decided, would be cheating.

I started asking fishermen to let me know if they found anything unusual in their nets. One gave me a pair of hogfish, snout-nosed, wine-colored species with yellow highlights that suggested spun gold. Satisfied at last, I spent a blissful month watching them glide through my tank. But one cool morning, when the temperature in the tank dropped a little too low, I found both of them floating on the surface, their fins limp, and their pale bellies pushing up as if seeking light.

A friend donated a mangrove snapper she had caught near a jetty. Normally purplish gray with iridescent red fins and a racy blue stripe through its eye, this fish turned pale yellow in the tank, as if scared witless by its incarceration. It too died. Finally, a friend who worked as an aquarist gave me a spadefish, a disc-shaped species with silvery sides and tapered stripes, like those on a zebra. Beneath the fluorescent light in my aquarium, its silky fins were tinged with purples and blues.

For two days I made excuses to spend time in the kitchen, just for the pleasure of watching the spadefish swim among my carefully arranged whelk shells and driftwood. On the third day, I noticed it wasn't eating. Small bits of cut fish lay scattered on the bottom of the tank, untouched.

I sprinkled some commercial fish food on the surface. The spadefish darted away. I dropped a few live mole crabs in the tank. It ignored them. Slightly worried, I turned back to my work. The next morning when I went to the kitchen for breakfast, I found the spadefish dashing itself against the back of the tank, its nose bruised and bloody red.

I grabbed a bucket and drained several gallons of water from the tank as the spadefish continued to beat itself against the glass. Near panic, I netted the fish, dropped it in the bucket, and ran with it to my car. I did not stop shaking until I reached the bridge over the clear waters of Oregon Inlet.

The spadefish was barely moving as I climbed over the rocky rip-rap along the shoreline to reach the deep water that lay beneath the bridge. It lurched sideways when I dipped the bucket in the ocean, but revived and quickly swam out. It turned sideways and paused, the slanted morning light illuminating its silver and black stripes, its amethyst fins. A second later it disappeared into the green depths.

The lessons of aquarium keeping, I think, mirror other lessons in life. Beware the showy and the beautiful, and take your pleasures from simple things.

Oregon Inlet, where Pamlico Sound empties into the sea, has become a place of solace for me, and I go there often. In midsummer, I like to stand on the boulders along the south shore so I can see down into the shadowed waters, where tropical fish swim in lazy schools. With a long-handled net, I could probably catch a few fish for my tank, but so far, I have resisted the temptation.

Instead, I have taken to picking up algae-covered rocks and oyster shells for the urchin to graze on and sea lettuce to feed half a dozen grass shrimp. This has unexpected benefits. Just as aquatic grasses provide food and shelter for scuds, oyster reefs harbor millions of tiny animals. One day I brought home a half dozen rocks and, without realizing it, a tiny blue shrimp. Released unnoticed with a swirl of new water into the tank, the shrimp burrowed into the gravel and began to grow. Months later, it announced its presence with a resounding SNAP!

I was home alone, doing the dishes. I turned off the water and spun around to survey the kitchen. I was not sure what I had heard. It sounded like someone clapping his or her hands. SNAP!

In a corner of the aquarium, in a tunnel between the under-gravel filter and the glass, was an inch-long, pale blue shrimp with one enormous claw. Its legs were coral and the fan of its tail had deep blue spots like those on a peacock's plume. More than a shrimp, it resembled a miniature lobster. As I watched, it opened its oversized claw, waved it toward a grass shrimp that hovered nearby, and popped it shut. SNAP! The grass shrimp flew backwards across the tank.

I learned later that the big-clawed snapping shrimp commonly burrows in oyster reefs. When threatened, it opens its large claw, creating a bubble that hovers in the water. As the claw snaps shut, water jets out of it at speeds of nearly sixty-five miles an hour, bursting the bubble and sending a tremendous POP through the water. Most would-be prey quickly retreat.

The presence of the snapping shrimp has given me reason enough for aquarium keeping; indeed, one whole winter I left the tank running solely for the sake of the shrimp, the urchin, and a few burrowing worms.

Sometimes I think it is as if those first scuds that traveled home in my pocket were a sign that I shouldn't hunt for marine animals, but simply enjoy whatever I happen to find. All summer I pick up rocks and oyster shells from the inlet, hoping they are covered with the spate and larva of marine animals. It is if my aquarium is an underwater garden and I am sowing seeds without knowing what they are. Unwittingly I have collected pipefish with bodies as thin as yarn, stone crabs with rounded purple claws, and flat-bottomed clingfish that slide over the glass walls, grazing on the algae that thickens every day.

Occasionally I still wish for some brightly spangled tropical fish that would swim around the tank rather than always groping along the bottom or climbing the sides. Yet I know now what happens to most tropical fish that grow up in the wild and are suddenly confined to amateur tanks:

they die. The stress of captivity is too much for them. Lately I have given up trying to create microcosms of beauty and have settled for authenticity. My aquarium is a first-class model of the coastal sounds, with their tepid, murky waters, slimy bottoms and sulfurous smells.

I have kept the aquarium for nearly a decade. Several years ago toward the end of the summer, a muddy gray, odd-looking fish appeared among the shells and stones I had scattered across the bottom of the tank. It was an inch long, with brown and olive flecks on its upper body and eyes as black and deep as the night sky. Its warty head took up nearly half its body, and its protruding lips turned downward in a permanent frown. Above each eye was a ridge that looked like part of a textured shell. It was an oyster toad, regarded by many fishermen as one of the ugliest creatures in the sea.

The toad tended to bury its body in stones and gravel with only the top of its oversized head exposed, then explode out to grab scuds or pieces of cut fish. At times it remained so motionless, I would prod it with a stick to make sure it was alive. I decided, for no reason, that it was a male and named him O.T. Gradually I came to think of him as beautiful: his fathomless eyes without pupils, his speckled, perfectly camouflaged coloration, his ridged eyebrows and fat frowning lips.

After he had lived with us for a year and a half and had grown to three inches, my husband confessed rather sheepishly, "I have learned to love an oyster toad."

O.T. died one fall after a pet store owner gave me some bad advice about mixing the water in my tank. For days afterwards I found it difficult to look at the aquarium. But winter was coming; I needed to collect more stones and shells so the urchin would have something new on which to graze. At Oregon Inlet once more, I couldn't help picking up several oyster shells, hoping that one would hold another toad.

My aquarium remains, to the unpracticed eye, little more than a pile of oyster shells and a piece of driftwood. Visitors dismiss it at a glance; some wonder aloud why I bother keeping it. I tell them I haven't had time to clean it, and seldom say more.

I keep the aquarium for study and diversion. I keep it, of course, for the urchin and the snapping shrimp. I keep it, finally, because it is so uncontrolled, a soup of invisible animals striving to grab hold of a niche and grow, grow with all their hearts, grow until they are big enough to be seen, big enough to fill their dark, scum-sullied, fragile, imperfect but infinitely beautiful world. ☙

This article first appeared in the Spring/Summer 2001 issue of *Outer Banks Magazine*.

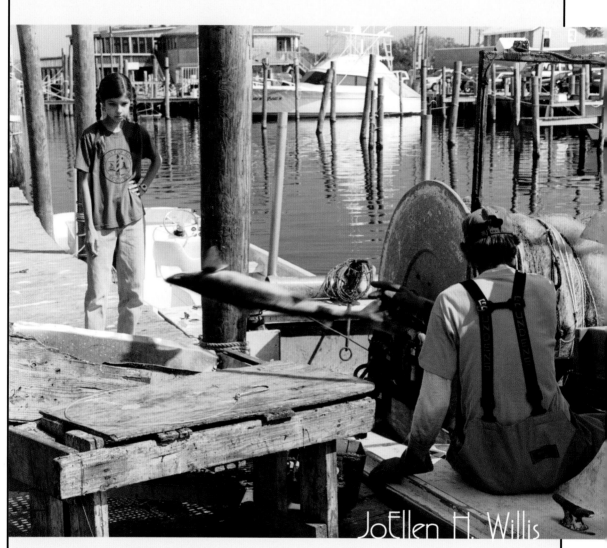

JoEllen H. Willis

JoEllen H. Willis is a photographer, wife and mother who spends the majority of her time trying to balance her dreams and ambition with the busy schedule of a typical American family. She spent her childhood in Hagerstown, Maryland, where her father introduced her to the joys of photography through recording the family history on film. She met her native-born husband, Bob, while working in Hatteras over a summer break from college.

The couple settled in the village permanently after JoEllen received a BA from the University of Delaware. For the past twenty years, she has been busy raising her family and squeezing in time to pursue her love for photography. Currently, she is operating a wedding and beach family portrait business, Silver Light Studio, as well as accepting free-lance work from local businesses, and is continuing to capture the beauty of the island with black and white landscapes.

Linda Elizabeth Nunn

After nearly half a century of doing the usual things an ordinary woman does, Linda Elizabeth Nunn came to Hatteras to begin life anew. She was a veterinary technician for twenty-five years, and is a freelance writer and editor, a teacher and a poet. She says her two daughters are her inspiration and guiding lights. Usually involved in several writing projects at a time, she treasures every single moment of life by the sea.

An Island of One's Own

Linda Elizabeth Nunn

I wrote my first poem when I was in the third grade. I remember sitting amidst a herd of sturdy shoes on the floor of my grandmother's bedroom closet, working on rhymes, translating the pictures in my mind to organized words on a yellow tablet. I toiled happily, oblivious to the world beyond the door. Mom read the poem at supper that night and I ate up the praise and mashed potatoes with equal satisfaction.

I moved on to writing one-act plays for my younger brothers to perform on Brooklyn playgrounds. When our family traveled to the backwoods of Tennessee, I found an enormous flat rock out behind the old barn and spent hours lying like a snake in the sun, writing stories of my new adventures. By sixth grade I was living in Ohio, and climbing neighborhood pine trees with pencil and notepad, struggling to keep my balance, and the resin from sticking my fingers to the paper. My thoughts flew as fast as the curious blackbirds circling my outpost.

High school opened the world to me. So much to learn, so many books to read, so many book reports to write! I discovered the classics, and acknowledged that reading took me happily out of my ordinary life while subtly teaching me the craft of writing.

I wrote poems at the request of friends, and though the subject was usually teenage angst and broken hearts, I plodded on. I ghosted homework assignments and term papers, and began keeping a journal. Still I sought private places to write: the fragrant, solemn attic, inside the neglected grape arbor, the back porch of an empty house down the street. I had yet to read Virginia Woolf's *A Room of One's Own*, but I instinctively knew I needed one.

Suddenly I was married, and though I usually found a corner for my desk in the succession of homes in which we nested, the demands of "housewifery" overcame my need to write. I sang lullabies to my infant daughters, and occasionally wrote one. Rhymes rolled through my head while I was shopping, scrubbing the bathtub, or dicing carrots. Carpooling, community activities, and entertaining my husband's business associates were all carried out while stories were born, died and were resurrected time and again. There were obligations to extended family, gardens to keep, dresses to iron, and children to guide and cherish. I attended to telephone calls, lists, meetings and appointments. I wondered how I could do it all when a job outside the home became necessary, but I managed the mayhem for nearly twenty years. Mothers, wives and daughters everywhere know of what I speak.

May Sarton writes, "One did one's work against a steady barrage of demands, of people… It was all very well to insist that art was art and had no sex, but the fact was that the days of men were not in the same way fragmented, atomized by indefinite small tasks. There was such a thing as woman's work and it consisted chiefly…in being able to stand constant interruption and keep your temper." Through all those years I kept my temper and quietly nourished my passion for writing when I could. During that time, I also made two life-altering discoveries: my growing need for personal freedom, and the magic and lure of the sea. I began to not-so-quietly nourish my yearning to have it all.

Soon, my daughters were grown and gone, the marriage was over, and I found myself in a Jeep with a large and very silly red dog, heading for the coast. Few people get a second chance in life, and fewer still, women. I grabbed mine with thrill and trepidation. Now I live on Hatteras Island,

with the ever-constant sea my companion to the east and south, and the great Pamlico Sound my neighbor north and west. In this new life, I am free to discover the realities of living on a barrier island, to find out who I am, to indulge my passion for the written word.

I live in an old cottage in the middle of a small village, and every single room is my own. Even with a well-appointed office, I often write at the kitchen table when the afternoon sun shining through lace curtains patterns my paper with intricate designs. Yet still I seek those special places, "rooms" where tangled thoughts weave themselves into place, where new ideas are born and thrive, where quandaries obediently resolve and questions beget more questions and finally answers. An island of one's own is generous to a hungry woman searching for the sacred and sublime.

I might sit in an old wooden chair by the pond, writing sonnets while the egret fishes for her breakfast. The live oaks with their Medusa limbs beckon me to climb, and dream. Propped against the remnant of a wisteria-covered fence, I write the final chapter of *Kristina in the River*. I meander along a deserted beach, listening to the surf rattling over the broken shells, and I absolutely know that Spanish moss is really mermaids' hair. I stop, pull my notepad from my pocket, and write the how and why of it for my future grandchildren.

For me, life here is as often difficult as it is euphoric. Learning to let go of old attitudes and negative habits in the face of a different and more appropriate lifestyle occasionally brings me up short. I still must be vigilant to avoid the hole in the ground, if I have not been smart enough to take another road altogether. My journal bulges with my private discussion of the changes in my life.

Fierce and ugly storms trounce the island, destroying sand dunes, washing out roads, prying off roofs, cutting our lines to the mainland. They bring the tide into the yards, flood low-lying homes, exhaust the wildlife, and test our patience, our courage, our endurance and our ability to rebuild. Sometimes, they threaten our very lives. With the power out, I write long letters by candlelight to my daughters, telling them how my house shudders in the furious wind, how I watch the tide rise to the very edge of the porch, how I have wrapped most of my precious possessions in plastic. I try to convince them not to worry, that I can survive here, knowing they will try to convince me to move to a safer location.

Realizing a responsibility to this exceptional place where I am certain I belong, I pay strong attention to the environment. I've watched the seasonal migrations of the birds, studied the winds, tides, and cycles of the moon, tested what grows in the garden and what gives in to the salt and the sand. I've noticed the slant of the cedars, the quiet vitality of the marshes, the movement of sandbars in the inlets, the erosion patterns on dunes and beaches, the debris piled up in the sheltered bays and channels of the sound. I write my observations in notebooks, and scrutinize the information so that I may live in harmony and with respect for the gifts that nature places in our hands.

Yet I also watch in dismay, and often anger, as acre after acre of trees are cut and shrub and wildlife habitat are plowed under and leveled by continuous and outrageous development. Having read the histories, and gently prodded reticent "old timers" to talk of the singular heritage of this extraordinary island, I see the treasured way of life here being violated with blatant disregard of the consequences. It is "my" island too, and I am compelled to do something. I do what I do best – I write about it.

Some say that writing is the loneliest of occupations, that the writer spends an inordinate amount of time alone, sequestered away, plying the craft. I disagree. Even if I seek the floor of a closet, I have a world of words and images before me. I have a crowd of characters to talk with, listen to, watch as they go about their business, do crazy things, do tender things. I have all the stars in the sky, all the fish in the sea, waiting as poems and prose, stories and songs, to appear beneath my pen.

If I stare at a blank page too long, if I am fragmented by indefinite small tasks, I have only to walk the beach at sunrise, listen to the gulls laugh, taste the salt on my lips. I am at once centered, renewed, strong and capable, and the words come. I am a fortunate woman, a woman who is a writer, and my "room of one's own" is an entire, precariously beautiful island. ❦

Cape of Hatteras

Linda Elizabeth Nunn

I will arise and go now, and go to Hatteras,
And a small house make there, of driftwood built.
A plot of sea oats will I have there, and a row boat,
And live alone on the sand dune hill.

And I shall have some peace there, for peace is slow,
Slow over the horizon, coming when the dawn sings.
There midnight is black velvet, and noon a furnace,
And evening full of seagull wings.

I will arise and go now, for always night and day,
I hear the ocean tumbling with mirth on the shore.
From maritime forest to windswept beach,
I hear it in my deep heart core. ☙

With regards to William Butler Yeats and *The Lake Isle of Innisfree*.

Hatteras Harmony

Linda Elizabeth Nunn

Listen…
Under a splendid sky, on this island away in the ocean,
a symphony – presented to the sun, to the moon.

Foaming surf creates a minuet upon a swale of broken shells,
with breakers rolling a flawless rhythm.

Laughing gulls call a humoresque as they wheel and dive
through the azure sky.

Foghorns moan a dirge for the ferries plowing the inlet
through dawn sea-smoke.

Raucous blackbirds chatter a toccata while tap dancing
through white cedars and live oaks.

Hurricane winds build to crescendo, shudder old windows,
beat boats lashed to the docks.

Out on the Point, the Labrador Current and the Gulf Stream
clash in a magnificent maestoso rhapsody.

A thousand snow geese gathered on the ponds of Pea Island
sing a resonant cantata on Christmas Eve.

Salted southwest breezes rustle a nocturne through marsh grasses,
swaying stands of sea oats and lithe oleander.

The voices of history, and the future, play a sustaining melody
along the back roads, through the channels and over the dunes
of this fragile strip of sand I call home. 🎼

Meanwhile

Dixie Browning

A sprouting seed can fell
A concrete wall.
A summer rain can
Trace a line
Across the earth,
That grows into a stream,
A riverbed.
The muscles of the ocean
Take the land and
Break the land and
Open a door
Where it would enter.

In spite of all
The Corps of Engineers
Can do.

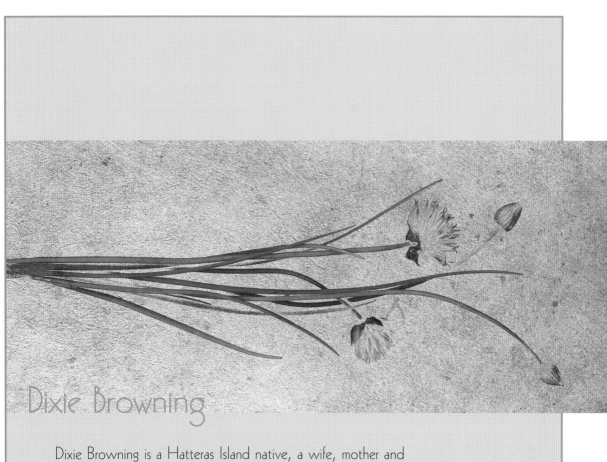

Dixie Browning

Dixie Browning is a Hatteras Island native, a wife, mother and grandmother. She is a painter, and was the first president of the Watercolor Society of North Carolina. Dixie is a prolific romance writer and the author of ninety-five published books to date.

Summer Monday

Dixie Browning

This time is mine,
This private hour
In my back yard.
My dreaming tower.
This hour was freshly
Bathed in rain,
Then dried by sun and
Wind again.
This cleanliness,
This clarity
Touches all the things
I see:
The tender green,
The sapphire blue,
The early yellow jonquils, too.
A bit of moss
On weathered gray,
A thrush's song,
A raucous jay.
I feel the earth's maternity.
A sense of peace envelops me.
A woman's ageless peace is mine,
While hanging clothes
On my clothes line.

Gee Gee Rosell

After college graduation in 1974, Gee Gee Rosell came to
Hatteras Island and earned her living by cleaning fish, painting
houses and fishing crab pots with her "companion of the moment."
She later worked for Eastern National Park and Monument
Association, and by the mid '80s opened Buxton Village Books in
an old island cottage. She wrote a monthly column for "The Island
Breeze" for ten years and still writes for the paper on occasion.
Gee Gee finds life today on the island nearly unrecognizable from
the vantage point of thirty years. However, she says life is good on
this stretch of sand despite her nostalgia for the early years. For
now, she is honing her perspectives and living one day at a time
with gratitude for the pleasures still to be found here.

Porches

Gee Gee Rosell

Porches come in all shapes and sizes: front porches, side or back porches, verandas, sleeping porches and utility porches. Screened porches are a necessity in the South where the weather encourages outdoor living but also breeds bugs that bite. Porches are evocative of a slower time – a time when folks sat on their front porches and visited with their neighbors in the evening.

Patios, palazzos and decks don't count as porches. A porch has to be a covered, sheltered, embracing sort of place. The porches in my life have been places where wonderful memories were made. My grandmother's front porch was a place where I sat surrounded by aunts and cousins and learned about this family of which I was part. It was where I later smoked my first cigarette and where I sat to say goodbye to my grandfather after his funeral. It was on that same grandmother's back porch where I had my first kiss. The front porch was way too public, but the back porch, with its swing and the sound of the crickets chirping, was just right.

My own parents' back porch was a place of wonder in my younger years. I can still smell the newly mown grass and see the stars start to twinkle in the deep navy summer sky and hear my mother's voice telling tales of Hiawatha or singing lullabies.

My house has a back porch, too. Sometimes I think that's why I bought that crazy little house. I liked the fact that it was a good safe place for my cats to live, but this house also has the most delightful hidden room. Except for the deep dark days of winter, my porch is my home. I eat, sleep and read there. I never, ever do work there. I didn't have to make that decision. It simply isn't a work sort of space.

While I'm writing this piece, my sister is sitting in my back porch swing reading a magazine and listening to Jimmy Buffett. Over the years innumerable friends and relatives have spent a night or a month on that porch. That's the kind of place a porch should be – a place to share summer things with the people you want in your life. That swing has rocked away my heartbreak and calmed my confusion. It's *circa* 1974, the first piece of furniture I ever bought, and has been moved with me at least a dozen times onto at least as many porches. It has great chunks missing where my horse chewed through the top rail. Every spring it gets a fresh coat of white paint.

My house is a small place, and the one suggestion I have heard since the first day I moved in from friends and neighbors is that I should enclose the screened porch to give myself more room. Well, there is room and there is "room." A porch provides room for the mind to wander and the dust to blow right on by. My porch doesn't need its windows washed or its closets cleaned. It's an unpretentious room that has only one wall but lots of ambiance. I can hear the mullet jump in the creek at midnight. I can watch the storm clouds roll in over the sound and sit through a pouring rain safe and dry. I can escape the blazing August heat without the chill of air conditioning.

Maybe we all try to recapture the best of our youth for the rest of our lives. The times we remember of peace and innocence before we knew about mortgages and insurance policies and drive-by shootings. If we're lucky, we can have that feeling again, even if only momentarily, and sometimes, I find those best of all feelings on my porch. ❦

Linda Meyer Browning

Linda Meyer Browning and her husband, Lou, own Browning Artworks, a gallery of North Carolina art and fine craft in Frisco. She is the American Red Cross Disaster Services Coordinator and Damage Assessment Team Coordinator for southern Hatteras Island. She is also a ham radio operator (K2LIN), involved with emergency communications. Browning is a member of Our Lady of the Seas Catholic Mission in Buxton where she is a lay minister and serves as a lector, minister of hospitality, and eucharistic minister. When she has time, she paints, capturing the island in watercolor.

Reflections on a Winter Night

Linda Meyer Browning

There is a lot to be said for living thirty miles out to sea. It awakens my senses and hones my awareness of my purpose in the cosmos. It stimulates my creativity and expands my curiosity. It bonds me to community and challenges my skill at survival. It makes me appreciate how tenuous my hold here is and makes my grasp stronger. It deepens my belief in God and calls me to be of help in meaningful ways.

Living thirty miles out to sea in *winter* gives me a chance to reconnect with all these things after keeping up with the frenzied pace of summer in the service sector. It gives me a chance to retune to the rhythms of nature. Winter gives me time to restore, refill, refresh, reflect, renew, repair, and rebuild.

On this winter evening, I am achingly aware that it won't be long before I will once again jerk spasmodically from one exhausting day to the next; when I'll flop on the couch after I get home from work and assume my customary "crash" position (back flat, head down, feet up); when the blood that pooled in my throbbing legs during the day will finally find its way back up to my brain and enable me to say to my husband, "So how was your day, babe?"; when I will melt into the couch and become the couch and not move for hours.

I am grateful. Exhaustion is good. It means that our business is thriving and throbbing with visitors on whom we depend for our livelihood. Many of them I love and long to see when they return next season. A few of them I hope never to see again. A thriving business means income, benefits, and retirement plans for us and the six other community members whom our business supports. I hope I'm exhausted next season, too, and the season after that.

I realize that the seasonal toll my busy life takes on my psyche dissipates as the winter deepens. I revel in the quiet and enjoy the sense of safety that this season brings. Hurricanes won't threaten for another half a year. I'm thankful for this respite, for it softens the sharp sadness I feel from seeing homes destroyed and lives turned inside out by the landfall of the visitors we fear. This interlude gives me a chance to blur the picture in my mind's eye of personal belongings heaped high along the roadside: furniture, clothing, appliances, children's toys, wedding albums, baby pictures, all ruined by storm tide and made worse by septic tank contamination. It dims the scenes of trash trucks hauling off bits of people's memories and pieces of their lives. Images of fist-size blooms of mold on the walls and ceilings of their flooded homes finally fade in my memory. I am an American Red Cross volunteer. Disaster Services work takes me into people's pain. I feel lucky. My losses have never been as great as my neighbors' losses.

Winter is the time of year when I join the other islanders in expelling one, long, collective sigh and retreat to the comfort of home. My family, friends, and faith community restore my supply of tolerance, understanding, patience and compassion with their nurturing. It's the time of year when residents carry on conversations from their trucks – they stop in the middle of the highway, windows rolled down, engines idling. No need to pull off the road. It's all but deserted.

Winter gives my husband and me a chance to refurbish our relationship with leisurely talks over morning tea and with long walks we now have time to take. It's the time when I rediscover the simple pleasure of playing with our dog, Skye, on the deserted beach. My senses seem specially honed for the winter season, and they record all its subtle nuances.

As I sit here listening to the sounds of my sleeping household, I too close my eyes and experience once more the day's magic on the beach with Skye. The light wind is out of the east. It's an unusual wind that typically brings rain. Instead of rain, it brings sea fog, a rare and wonderful phenomenon that drifts toward me on the moist air and the wings of a gull. It wafts in from the ocean and wraps surf sounds in wool. It fills my ears with cotton. It paints my glasses white, and Skye disappears into the veil in front of me. His leash is taut, and I cannot see him. Some invisible entity pulls me down the beach. As the fog tiptoes past me on its journey west, I detect the sweet scent of sea grape. I can't see the dunes, but I know they're close. I can smell them. I inhale deeply. Now I can also smell the dry smoke grass, broom sedge, and sea oats that give the balmy salt air a pungent, earthy smell. Small things of the sea are trapped and lie dying in the high tide line of debris at my feet.

Suddenly Skye's leash goes slack. He has halted his energetic stroll to sniff at a dead shark half buried in the sand. Its desiccated body has been here for weeks and no longer smells of rotting flesh. Skye's leash goes taut once more as he moves down the beach in search of fresher flotsam. My mind moves on to other things.

Winter days bring me Van Gogh dawns. They bring fishermen giant tuna. They bring loons in breeding plumage and gannets in huge numbers. They bring the cries of broad-winged hawks and osprey that prepare for their next round of nesting. Winter days bring robins and cedar waxwings that arrive side by side by the hundreds and fill the woods with springtime song. These migrating travelers stay only as long as it takes for them to eat their fill of berries that bend low the evergreens around my house. The birds then leave as quickly as they come. Suddenly the woods are still. Silence is restored.

This season's sunsets are gifts wrapped in garish pinks and gold, purples and ultramarine blue. The skyscapes are textured with Gulf Stream clouds grazing along the horizon like herds of sheep. Doves, cardinals, and common yellowthroats – the birds of day – snuggle under their blankets of yaupon and myrtle as the canopy grows dark. Dusk yields to night.

The night hides the spore of uncaring and thoughtless humans. Beer bottles and soft drink cans hurled out of passing cars, candy wrappers and plastic grocery bags blown out of pickup trucks, all fade into the embracing purple shadow. Like a layer of fresh snow, darkness covers that which assaults my love and pride of this place. The colorful, shiny scat eventually will find its way into our waters, strangling sea turtles with cellophane, ponytail keepers and plastic. I will pick up what I can tomorrow when the morning light reveals this blight. I will leave the road kills to others on the food chain.

I turn my eyes heavenward. Orion, Cassiopeia, Pleiades, the Big Dipper, Venus and Jupiter monopolize my view, which is made all the more spectacular by the clarity of the cold night air. Even the tiniest pricks of light sparkle with diamond brilliance. I think of God shining his bright light behind the black velvet curtain that is textured with pinholes. I watch a satellite glide toward the moon.

The nocturnal world of winter welcomes the occasional calls of great horned owls looking for mates. Some of the island's single men look also. A few choose "winter women" to share their beds until the girls of summer return. No promises are offered. No commitments are requested. For them, the winter is too long. For me, it is not long enough. All too soon the highway will be crowded with cars once again. The roadside will be littered with even more waste of "civilization." The beach will be salted with white coolers and peppered with tanned bodies. All too soon I will steel myself for another season of grateful exhaustion and pray for a benign storm season.

For now, I shall enjoy the tranquility of winter.

Tonight is remarkably quiet. From my living room, I can hear the breakers playing their crescendos on the distant beach. The wind is calm, as is my mind. The highway is quiet, as is my soul. The island rests, as do I. 🐾

Mary Talley

Mary Talley lived in Frisco from 1977 to 2001. Her writing
has appeared in "The Island Breeze," Icarus International's poetry
competition chapbook, and "The Dead Mule." She has been an
active member of the Dare Writers' Group, the Frisco Civic
League and the Hatteras Island Friends Meeting. Kite flying,
ducks and good friends have been special to her here.

My Empty Nest

Mary Talley

It was going to be one of the hardest things about leaving Sea Note, my home for twenty-three years, and I wanted to do it without distraction and rush. So relocating the ducks, letting them go, was what I did as soon as we got the contract for the purchase of our house.

I was glad in some ways that the people who were buying the house, even though they love ducks and have raised them, said they would not be able to keep them because they wouldn't be living here full time for a while. They have a dog, and I don't trust even trustworthy dogs with ducks.

More than that, I wanted to find a just-right place for those very special beings in my life. Harry Willis, a neighbor and "duck friend," told me about giving ducks to the restaurant managers at the Castaways Motel in Avon. Bettie, my partner, immediately caught the appropriateness of that name. It's a good thing she did; I wasn't laughing about anything related to the matter.

One little exchange with Betty Horan at the restaurant did wonders for easing my heart. She sparkled with excitement when I asked how it would be if I brought seven ducks to the pond on the grounds there. "That would be wonderful! And I feed them year round," she said. Her manner as she spoke of the other ducks already there clearly conveyed her caring and appreciation for ducks.

The pond itself is perfect – surrounded by a five-foot-deep hedge of reeds with a convenient gap at one end of a large oval of fresh water. The reeds provide spaces for nesting and protection from sun, loose dogs and pestering people, plus lots of natural food even if Betty didn't give them daily rations of cracked corn. There are turtles in the pond, but our ducks are turtle wise.

So it was obvious; that is where the ducks would relocate. But how? I've never handled them or petted them and getting them all into a vehicle that could move them sixteen miles up the island – past the relocated Cape Hatteras Lighthouse and beyond the first traffic light south of Whalebone Junction – without terrifying them into shock or permanently fouling whatever conveyance they were in, was a challenge for me which had some parallels to that faced about the same time last year by the International Chimney and Expert House Movers.

It came to me that when Harry Willis had given us ducks over the years, he'd often used tow sacks. While the ducks resisted being put into the burlap, they were quite calm once they were inside and the top was well tied.

Cardboard boxes are easier to come by. I hied me to the ABC store and selected seven premium brand carriers – Johnny Walker Black, Wild Turkey, Absolut, Bombay – nothing but the best for our ducks!

Barbara Nash, a gentle, gracious friend and neighbor, who for years has cared for the ducks when we have been away, responds to their specialness with appreciation and devotion. She came early the morning of the relocation to help. I needed her every inch of the way – spreading the plastic drop cloth over the cargo area of the Raider, coaxing Bert, the 'scovie drake (who lived outside the pen because of his size), into the pen where we could catch him, catching the ducks by hand or with a landing net.

Barbara and I, in turn, would catch a duck, put it into a liquor box, fold the flaps and step out of the pen where Bettie stood ready to spread duct (yes!) tape over the top. Then when that box was in the Raider, we'd go back into the pen with another box and repeat the procedure. We were all cautious not to scare or hurt the ducks, who were understandably startled, and we wanted to avoid slipping or kneeling in the abundant supply of fresh manure provided during the stress of the feathered ones. We were a good team and even in that confined space, succeeded on both those counts.

The ducks, even the two who are not muscovies and can quack very effectively, were quiet as we drove up the road. Barbara and I were too. After we parked near the pond at Castaways, Betty, her husband, Bill, and their son came out of the restaurant. As Barbara and I set the boxes out near the gap in the reeds, Bill lightened our mood by observing, "Honey, looks like we've got some boot-leggers here." Betty really warmed my heart as we opened box after box. She exclaimed with genuine pleasure when each duck was released, "Oh, how beautiful," or, "Look at that one!" She truly liked them.

I let Bert out of his box first. He'd been alpha duck for a couple of years and I knew the others would fly to him. Bert flew immediately to the far end of the pond. The others were none the worse for their transit and readily stretched their wings and flew to join Bert, swimming and exploring the pond.

I was so pleased to see how at ease the ducks were, and to feel the reassurance of Betty's appreciative exclamations, that it took me some time to acknowledge other aspects of the reality of what had just happened.

The ducks and I would never again putter together in the yard. I'd not get to see their eggs or gather some of them for our kitchen, or enjoy the ducks' zest when earthworms fell out of the bin where we compost kitchen scraps, or watch their cooperative response when I rattled the can of cracked corn near the door of the pen

More than all that, and harder to describe, I'd forever miss the pleasure of their trust and presence. Over the years, during the daily rhythm of my letting them out of the pen in the morning and shepherding them back in by late afternoon, they had taught me to think like a duck.

They tend to lay their eggs at first light. If they stayed out of the pen at night, in the morning they naturally nested in secluded places in the woods or the marsh. Since a duck won't abandon her eggs, both were fully vulnerable to raccoons and other predators. "Sitting duck" is not a casual metaphor.

Getting the ducks back into the pen in good daylight became an important part of the daily routine. They liked the pen. It was their safe place; it had good nest boxes, pans of fresh water, often luscious leaves of lettuce.

Even so, going through a door is a hard step for a duck to take. It goes counter to some instinctive cautions – and my anxiety in the beginning about "helping" must surely have added to their uneasiness.

I know a few of the ways that made it easier for them to go into the pen, but I think the treasured thing that happened to me was that we took a step beyond familiarity and routine. I came to recognize variations in their patterns and to accommodate their paths and timing, and they came to trust my signals. We learned to dance together.

In recent years getting the ducks back into the pen has become as easy as – well, as water rolling off a duck's back. Daily as it was, each time I felt a specialness in the routine of trust. I always knew that they did it because they wanted to.

There's an ironic twist to all this. The day after the great relocation event, our realtor called to say that the prospective buyer had withdrawn his offer. But the deed of duck moving had been done; undoing it would have been very complicated. Of course, we still hoped for a prompt sale of our house to someone else.

That was three months ago. The ducks still act as if they remember me when I visit them in their new home. The most recent treat was Betty's call that Gladys has hatched ten babies and Dawn had four. All seven Sea Note ducks have survived, thanks in large to Betty's prodigious efforts of retrieval when some flew the first couple of days and couldn't find their way back to the pond. Folks in Avon know Betty's affinity for ducks and call her any time they see one in an unaccustomed setting. She even spotted one of ours from a restaurant window as it wandered in a dune by the beach, and went out in the course of serving meals to bring it back to the pond! Her customers were understanding.

For three months now there have been no ducks at Sea Note. I still expect to see them when I'm in the yard and watch for them when I back the car around. I no longer catch myself setting aside lettuce leaves for them or making plans to change their water. That daily routine was a truly special experience. I don't expect to have another like it.

I don't need to. 🪶

Since Mary wrote this story, the Castaways has been demolished, the pond plowed over, and new construction dots the area. Mary's ducks and their new companions were relocated once again to another safe place in Avon.

To the Mink Who Killed Three Ducks in a Pen Where I'd Contained Them for Protection

Mary Talley

From a distance I see your unfamiliar form.
Pretty, lithe, you bounce easily in and out of the wire enclosure,
Leaving only as I draw near.

This time: dear old Willene, still breathing her last breaths,
Blood flowing fast from her neck, which
You've completely stripped of feathers and skin.

I fortify the pen against you.

Next day: beautiful champagne-feathered Trice
And her mate, bright Thursday,
Whose neck you pull out
Through the one remaining gap, so narrow his body stays inside.
Their cold abused forms await my arrival.
Remaining ducks, stunned, mute, defenseless
In a pen of muck, residue of your effective work.

My heart, skinned, scraped,
Hurts like a child falling hard on gravel,
Too far from home to cry.

Three dear ones die because
You are so good at what you do.

Eight shocked survivors still follow me
With trust and expectation of my care.

May I do as well as you. 🦆

Michal Schliff

Michal Schliff was a native North Carolinian who spent her life in an eclectic mix of careers. She was a Peace Corps volunteer in Turkey, where she met her husband, Henry. After the Peace Corps, the Schliffs taught school in New York City and eventually a summer job on Cape Cod led them to discover their love for cooking. They cooked at Cape Cod and Palm Beach, and eventually in Chapel Hill, North Carolina, where Michal enrolled in the PhD program at the University of North Carolina. A restaurant business venture led them to Nags Head and eventually Hatteras Island, where they bought the Orange Blossom Bakery in Buxton in 1991. Michal immediately settled into life on Hatteras, working at the bakery with Henry and their son, and writing for "The Island Breeze," the island's monthly newspaper. Michal had a very personal relationship with Hatteras, which, she said, gave her a sense of what was really important in life. She died in November 2000, after a two-year struggle with breast cancer. As she had requested, her ashes were scattered on the beach at Cape Hatteras Lighthouse, her favorite spot to walk and reflect, on the winter solstice, December 22, 2000.

The Gift of Light
The Story of One Woman's Love for the Lighthouse

Michal Schliff

December is the season for stories, stories of magic and miracle, stories of creation and caring, stories of benevolence and birth, of promise and possibility, stories of the dreams we dream, of the hopes that flitter dove-like in our hearts longing to burst free and fly. Most of all, December is the season for stories of light, the light of Hanukkah candles burning bright, the pathfinding light of Bethlehem's star, and the glow of our lighthouse shining again in the winter sky, joining its beam with the stars and the moon to light our way.

I would like to tell you my own December light story, which began I don't know exactly when – perhaps sometime soon after my family and I decided to buy a bakery and move to Buxton. This was in January of 1991, when the Bonner Bridge was out. (A section was damaged by a dredge in October of 1990.) We traveled from Chapel Hill to Nags Head where we spent the night. By dawn the next day, we were waiting at the ferry dock to make the trip across Oregon Inlet. We waited and waited until the fog finally lifted, then we boarded the ferry and spent what seemed like a small eternity skirting sandbars in the sound. At last we arrived on Pea Island and zipped down the island toward Buxton in order to sign the contract that would change our lives.

For several years we had had a vacation cottage in Hatteras Village. I had always loved the beauty of Hatteras. I wasn't so sure about Buxton. The word that came to mind when I thought of it was an old hippy term: funky. As for the Cape Hatteras Lighthouse, I never really thought of it at all. We had made the obligatory visit with our young son, and we had uttered the usual comments about how lovely it looked in its setting beside the sea. We even took a picture from the big turtle pond with the lighthouse posing behind the trees on the far shore.

It was during the spring of 1991 when my husband and I were taking turns commuting between Chapel Hill – where we still had a business – and Buxton that the lighthouse first began to take on meaning in my life. After spending the weekend in Chapel Hill with my family, I would return to the Outer Banks alone for another week's work in the bakery. By the time I reached Avon on Sunday evening, it would be dark. As I headed down the stretch of road from Avon to Buxton my thoughts would turn to my husband and son. Just as I began to feel the loneliness and the blackness of the night closing in, the lighthouse beacon would catch my attention. As I continued down the road, I would count the seven point five seconds aloud and there the light would be again – regular and true. It didn't take many trips before I began to look forward to being greeted by the lighthouse beam in the night sky. I soon came to feel that it was welcoming me home.

During our first summer at the Orange Blossom, my husband and son and I looked forward to spending each evening out at the lighthouse beach, playing in the tidal pools, body surfing in the waves, walking our dog along the shore – all of this beneath the benign gaze of what we inevitably came to consider "our" lighthouse. We always stayed for the sunset. As the cool evening descended, we would lie in the water, which felt deliciously warm, and we would watch, with a combination of contentment, joy, and awe, the moving picture of the sun turning over its reins to the lighthouse for the hours of the night.

Within a few years our business changed, our son grew older, and it was no longer convenient to spend those early evening hours together at the lighthouse beach. There came a summer of trouble when our son was in his mid teens. Not knowing what to do or how to help, when to speak, when to remain silent, I began going to the lighthouse on my own. Ostensibly, I was walking our dog, but really I was going out to the lighthouse to pray – not to the lighthouse but within its presence, for I felt there in the midst of such beauty – at the meeting point of sky and sea – God could not be far away. I cherished the comforting presence of my old and familiar friend, my lighthouse.

I walked the grounds at different times of the day and night, but my favorite time, and most consoling, was the dusk, for then I would see the beam as it first came on for the night. Invariably, I felt the lighthouse light brightening and lightening my soul.

Our family's times of trouble passed, not without heartache and struggle, but we made it through to the other side together. Our son began to grow and thrive, and we entered a new and busy period of our lives as he decided to take karate classes in Kitty Hawk. Karate was something we had done together in Chapel Hill when he was a young child. Now he was determined to earn his black belt. But he didn't have a driver's license. Since I would be driving him up the beach, I decided that it would be a fine thing if I earned a black belt with him. What a rich memory it would make, participating in this once-in-a-lifetime experience with my son. For a year we made the drive to and from Kitty Hawk three nights a week. Usually by the time we passed back through Avon at 9:30 at night, I felt a bone-deep weariness. My son, too, was physically tired, but he was mentally buoyant and alert. Together we looked for our beacon of light, and there it would be, lighting us home, week after week. "There's the light!" I would always announce, feeling the need to say it aloud.

One night on our way home, the fog was so dense that we couldn't see the light shining anywhere along the route from Avon to Buxton. When we reached Old Lighthouse Road, I felt so worried that I actually turned and drove out to make sure something hadn't happened to the lighthouse. Partway down the road, we saw the beam, shortened and splintered by the fog, but still shining.

By the time of our black-belt test in late November of 1998, I was beginning to feel somewhat splintered myself. My tiredness just wouldn't go away. Well, I told myself, who wouldn't feel tired working eight hours a day, six days a week, and then training three nights a week with physically fit people less than half my age?

Somehow or other, I clawed my way awkwardly but ultimately with ragged triumph, through the weekend-long test, while my son flew through the ordeal with grace and skill. I received the great gift of experiencing this time of challenge with my only child, who was now a young man.

We had half-planned to spend that Christmas with my husband's brother, Jim, and sister-in-law Barbara in Schenectady, New York, but then decided to stay home. I didn't feel like so much traveling after the exhausting test. Our son now had his driver's license and could get to and from Kitty Hawk on his own. He continued making the trip three nights a week. I dropped back to two nights, and then as winter turned to spring, one night seemed all that I could manage. From Schenectady, we heard the worrisome news that Barbara's breast cancer had returned, after ten years of good health. She seemed to be responding well to treatments. As always, when we spoke on the phone, her voice was bright and warm and filled with hope and cheer.

By late spring I was aware of the lump in my left breast. I denied it at first. Lying in bed at night, I would gingerly touch the spot, then snatch my hand away. *This can't be.* But it was. I dropped out of the karate class. For two weeks I stayed quiet, gathering strength. I did yoga balancing poses, for I knew I would need good balance in the time to come. I went to the lighthouse and sat on the big sandbags with the lighthouse at my back. I inhaled the clean, fresh salt air and basked in the stream of early morning sunlight flowing across the sea to meet me. I strolled slowly through the lighthouse shadow that cut across the spring-green lawn. With each step, I prayed for guidance and for strength. Then I went to see a doctor.

In the Kitty Hawk office where I sat waiting for a follow-up X-ray after I was told that I was going to have to undergo a mastectomy, I looked at a painting of the Cape Hatteras Lighthouse on the office wall as the tears rolled down my cheeks and throat and onto the breast that I was going to lose. I cried and cried, all the while looking at the lighthouse painting and saying to myself, "I can do this. I can do this." The lighthouse painting watched over me, holding me in its light.

After the surgery in Norfolk, I sat in the breast surgeon's office. Here was another painting of the Cape Hatteras Light. I gazed at it as the surgeon informed me that all of the lymph nodes under my arm had been cancerous. He had removed them. As he spoke of treatment options – aggressive chemotherapy, extensive radiation, both of which might help to "buy time," as he put it – I studied the lighthouse painting. This view of the lighthouse was different from any I had ever seen. The artist, instead of painting from an onshore perspective, showed the view from the sea. It was as if the artist had walked out on the water to look back at the land. It seemed appropriate, as I thought of it. After all, those who truly needed the light were the ones who were out at sea – not those on the land.

I kept the painting with me in my heart and mind in the following weeks as I began to develop a different outlook. I underwent one chemotherapy treatment, then decided it wasn't what I wanted to do. I stepped out on the sea to look at my life from a wider, richer, deeper perspective. From that vantage point, I found the courage to say "no" to expectations and "yes" to my own vision, my own light, which I was just beginning to realize was something that lived inside of me.

It was now September of 1998. My sister-in-law Barbara's condition was worsening. I wanted to visit her, but I knew in my heart that there wouldn't be time, so I went out to the lighthouse and traveled the grounds. I imagined her walking with me on that bright blue day. A few days later, we drove to Schenectady for her funeral Mass. I thought I was going in order to try to be of some support to her husband, Jim, but as it turned out, along with the other mourners, I was going to receive a gift.

The Mass was a lovely tribute to a rich and loving life. Toward the end of the service, the priest waved an incense burner over the top of the closed casket, which was bathed in the rainbow-colored light cast on it from the enormous stained-glass window at the rear of the church. A large, silvery smoke ring formed at the end of the casket. Slowly the elegant smoke ring rose, keeping its circular shape as it drifted higher, passing just over Jim's head. As the entire congregation watched, it elongated into the shape of a woman's long flowing gown, which traveled through the rainbow light, merging with and then slowly dissolving into it. I left the service feeling that I had been blessed with the gift of being with Barbara one more time.

Back in Buxton there was talk of the coming lighthouse move. I felt torn. I wanted the lighthouse saved; I also wanted it to stand in that spectacularly beautiful setting where I had always known it to be – at the meeting point of sky and sea. In the next months, I followed the move in haphazard and sporadic fashion. I couldn't stand seeing the beautiful grounds torn up, so I stayed away. I couldn't tolerate not visiting the site where I had found so much solace and inspiration, so I went again to bear witness to the destruction, which seemed to me to amount to desecration. As the lighthouse was severed from its foundation, I walked beneath its base to touch the underside of it, and I realized that I identified this "surgery" with my own surgery, this upheaval with the radical changes in my own life, the new base with the reconstruction I had undergone. As the months passed and the Herculean efforts of International Chimney and Expert House Movers succeeded in speeding the lighthouse along the track to its new home, I realized that I also identified with this movement to and for survival. I wanted this continuation for the lighthouse, even in its limited new setting, just as I wanted my own survival. Of course, to state the obvious, I am a person and the lighthouse is a man-made structure. But I think my feelings have not been so very different from the intense emotional involvement shown by thousands of people who have wanted the lighthouse saved, either where it was or in its new location.

After the move was complete, I continued to visit the old site, but I did not traipse back through the woods to the claustrophobia-inducing new grounds. I preferred to view my old friend from a distance. After half a year of looking at the puny red warning lights atop it, I got to the point where I thought I didn't even miss the beacon.

A week before the relighting ceremony was to take place, Jim drove down from Schenectady with his sister, Gert. They arrived with so many presents, we thought it was Christmas in November, a feeling that was intensified by the fact that three of the gifts were actually wrapped in Christmas gift paper. Jim explained that he had been going through closets and had come upon these wrapped and labeled gifts. There was one for each of us. The handwriting on the gift labels was Barbara's. Jim had no idea what the boxes contained. With some trepidation, he handed each of us one of Barbara's gifts. Our son's present was a handsome shirt that fit perfectly. My husband opened a box containing a framed portrait of a smiling Barbara surrounded by her family. I was the last to open my gift, for I was so struck by the familiarity of the little figure on the label that I sat staring at it. It was an angel in a long flowing gown, blowing on a golden trumpet – an exact replica of the shape formed by Barbara's smoke ring as it merged with the rainbow light. Feeling that the label itself was gift enough, I opened the package anyway to find – lighthouses. There were four matted photographs of the Outer Banks lighthouses. As we looked at the lovely photographs, Jim figured that Barbara must have bought them on her final visit to Hatteras Island and put them aside to give to us on that Christmas when we were supposed to visit Schenectady.

Now here we were coming around to another Christmas, and we had our gifts from Barbara, as fresh and timely as if she had just wrapped them and written our names above hers on the Christmas label.

In the following week, as the date for the relighting of the lighthouse approached, I thought about Barbara's gift, of how she had chosen to give me pictures of all the Outer Banks lighthouses and not just the one photo of the Cape Hatteras Light, which she knew I loved. I thought about the lighthouse – lighthouses – as symbols of the light we are each capable of carrying within ourselves to light the way, not only for ourselves but also for our friends and families and strangers in our midst in times of crisis and danger, trouble and darkness, separation and grief.

On the afternoon of Saturday, November 13, my husband and I talked about making plans to see the relighting ceremony. In truth, neither of us could work up much enthusiasm for standing in a crowd, listening to speeches. So, at a little after 5 p.m., we stepped out on our bakery porch, where, thanks to the move of the century, we now have a perfect view of the top of the lighthouse. We watched the light flash on.

"Well," I said, "Let's dash out to Ramp 43 and watch it from the beach."

My husband was skeptical. "The crowds?" he murmured.

"We'll zip out," I said, "while they're on their way back from the ceremony."

Of course, as with most of my spur-of-the-moment strategies, things worked out otherwise. Cars were parked on both sides of the road from Highway 12 to the campground. As dusk settled into darkness, we crept along in our car while people swarmed all over the road. Our headlights illuminated all manner of people – smiling, frowning, babbling, disgruntled, people meandering, people rushing. A woman blithely ignored the fact that her little dog was roaming into our path. A father shepherded his young boys along. An elderly woman boldly strode in front of us, waving her arms like a traffic cop as she held up the line to allow her husband to barrel out into the road. So many people.

"I've never seen so many people," my husband said at one point.

At last we reached the turn-around area just past Ramp 43. The traffic that was trying to get

back to Highway 12 was backed up by this time nearly
to the ramp. With our dog, we got out of our car and
headed out to the beach where we joined with a crowd
of people, who, like us, had decided to enjoy this view
of the lighthouse. The sliver of a waxing moon shone
bright in the sky. We walked the beach for a while,
then found a slab of broken asphalt to sit on while we
gazed up at the stars. We thought we saw a satellite
blipping by. It could have been an airplane high in the
sky. Whatever it was, it was fun to see it weaving a trail
among the stars. The scent of someone's marijuana
drifted in our direction. We caught flashes of light
as fishermen cast their lines. We heard laughter and
children's excited cries as a group of them, for some
reason, decided to heft and carry home one of the big
chunks of broken pavement. The lighthouse beam
shone over us all.

Shoulder to shoulder, we sat in the light of the
moon and stars and our lighthouse. "This is a good
place to wait," my husband said.

Along with the thousands of people who had come
out to witness the turning-on of the light, I felt a
sense of gladness to see the beacon shining in the
night sky. I recognized that symbols are, after all,
important. But the ultimate value of the lighthouse –
of all lighthouses – I now understood, lay in the
hearts of all of us who have come to take the light
into our hearts. It was a gift to receive, and then to
give. It was the gift of light.

This story was first published in *The Island
Breeze*.

Susan West

Susan West is a freelance writer who has lived
on the Outer Banks for twenty-seven years.
A native of Maryland, she is married to a
commercial fisherman and is active in fisheries
management. Susan is the vice president of
the Hatteras-Ocracoke Auxiliary of the
North Carolina Fisheries Association.

For Ruthy and Her Husband

Susan West

I was meant to have been born in an earlier time and I've known that all my life. I might have gone west in a covered wagon, might have been a sodbuster on the plains, might have labored to tame the great American wilderness.

But I was born in the middle of the twentieth century and I live a mostly modern life. My husband is a fisherman though, and his occupation summons up earlier times when Americans worked with the sea and the soil and were as much a part of the natural world as the fish, the beaver, or the deer.

My husband and I live by nature's clock. Weather alternatively blesses us and then deals us a string of harsh blows. Our calendar is marked by patterns of migration, by seasons. There's Spanish mackerel season, blue crab season, seasons for trout and croaker.

My husband pulls nets full of fish out of the sea with consonant grace. That was meant to be. Fish were meant to be taken from the sea. But conservationists believe they know the sea and its creatures better than we and now cast a critical eye on the fisherman and his nets. The conservationists say, "The fisherman can't see the big picture. He only sees his little patch of the sea." Condescension implodes what should be a natural alliance between the fisherman and the conservationist.

We find few allies among recreational fishermen. Their political prophets wage a winner-take-all strategy, seeking to have all the fish, seeking to increase the already lucrative trade in the symbols of leisure – not just rods and reels but fast and faster boats, condos at the beach, and SUVs. A turtle or a whale is caught in a net and the recreational mob screams that the use of nets must cease.

Ruthy, also married to a commercial fisherman, visited a Web site frequented by recreational fishermen. I don't know Ruthy but few women log onto the site and I paid close attention to her posts. Ruthy wrote, "There are things in the fishing industry that might need changing. But there is no need to poke fun at these men. I watch my husband day by day get worse from arthritis. His hands and feet go dead on him. Help to change those things that need changing but please have a little compassion. We all have just a few days on this earth. God have mercy on us all."

The response to Ruthy's request for a little compassion? One recreational fisherman wrote, "Ruthy, along with a lot of her commercial friends, are out of touch with reality. They think we are supposed to get all 'weepy' when a person goes out wasting the resource to feed his family. Let him work at the 7-11."

Another wrote, "If your job is morally wrong, then get another."

Still another wrote, "Your lame justifications with religious references disgust me. Need more money? Get another job. Stop the senseless killing and encourage the other money grubbers to do the same."

Ruthy's husband trawls for flounder, a legal method of netting fish. Yet on this particular judgment day in cyberspace, Ruthy's husband is condemned as a senseless murderer and a moneygrubber, working at a morally wrong job and wasting the resource.

I suspect that many of the recreational fishermen hurling vials of hatred are pawns in a war they don't understand. Will the recreational fisherman be better off if there are no commercial fishermen? Will he catch more fish? Bigger fish? Better fish? Will he have more fun? Will he be happier?

It's obvious that the commercial fisherman will lose if nets are outlawed, but the working stiff who just wants to unwind with his rod and reel on the fishing pier won't be the winner either. I won't know any of the winners. They run with a different crowd than the people who live or vacation here.

Hatteras Island will lose as another speck of coastal character is wiped away. The children and grandchildren of fishermen, whether they be plumbers or builders or tackle shop owners, will lose the fiber of their heritage, which will no longer make sense.

When I'm an old woman, the children will whisper, "She was born in a time, long ago, when there were fishers of men." ⚓

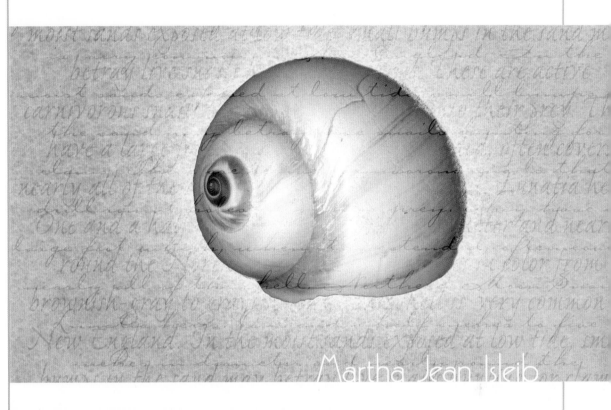

Martha Jean Isleib

Martha Jean Isleib is an avid gardener, a musician, a healer, a risk-taker, an insatiable
reader, an artist, a mother of two, grandmother of two, a lover of animals, a sister, a
daughter, a friend to many, a seeker of life's truths. Exploring and understanding the
many dimensions of living on the earth — its geography, its people, its history, its
wonders and its magic — is her life's work. She has known and loved Hatteras Island
since she was in diapers. She has been a resident off and on since 1976, having lived
in Hatteras, Buxton (on a boat), Frisco and Avon. She owns a home in Frisco, where
her daughter happily resides with her loving husband and two fine sons (and where
Martha intends to return at will in the not-too-distant future to enjoy island life).
Martha currently lives in Chapel Hill, where she is developing her business as a licensed
massage therapist amidst a plethora of diverse cultural experiences, while her
16-year-old son, Zachary, attends high school.

The Healing

Martha Jean Isleib

I once had it explained to me, quite matter-of-factly, as it were, that the people who are drawn to spend a portion of their lives here on the island consistently come from a place of deep pain and dysfunction. They are secretly spirited here, to be soothed and healed, lulled by the vastly fluctuating rhythms of the sea. At times, so intense and raw as to match the soul of the deepest griever and then so utterly calm and peaceful, barely a ripple beneath, or on the surface . . . mirroring the times of grace bestowed upon each in due season.

Footsteps of the seeker wander aimlessly,
stopping here and there to examine a treasure waiting to be found,
to be coveted and secreted away as a remembrance of the moment,
washed over again and again by the incoming tide,
until there is no evidence that any such feet were ever really there,
and all the while, a subtle transformation is occurring,
the spirit is renewed, the mind quieted, the flesh refreshed.

Breathing in the pure essence of the salt water,
so akin to our own life's blood,
undoubtedly saturating each being's lungs
with a unique combination of its healing properties,
countless minute essential nutrients to be sent
pulsing through the arteries,
rhythmically, rhythmically,
as the waves in unending succession bathe the shoreline,
and with the simplicity of breathing,
absorbing that which is depleted and desperately craved.
So heals the sea.

Lying on the beach in the sun,
the sand absorbing every last flicker of tension,
while gulls whirl and call,
the crash of the curls resounding in tireless rhythmic disposition.
Molded to the earth itself, so fully connected as to feel
a sense of completion unmatched by any other repose,
a sense of belonging, a cradling effect,
safe at the edge of the mother's womb.
Until the beating of the sun becomes intolerable
for even a single moment longer,
and you find yourself propelled by some mystical unmistakable force,
legs in motion, toward the water, ever drawn toward the water;

perhaps a dip of the toe,
to allow a moment's preparation for the plunge, the intense plunge,
into the sea, timed perfectly with the flow.

Then to be engulfed . . . ah, the pleasure unsurpassed,
pure joy, unadulterated,
unable to feel just exactly where skin separates from ocean,
being taken, as a lover,
perhaps in gentle caresses, then again,
with exhilarating power,
until all thought ceases and the mind, body and spirit are
cleansed to perfection.

Yes, I can see it. We come to be healed, as the sea washes clean the earth, filtering out impurities,
so it, too, restores us to our very core. As for the deep grief and dysfunction, I must agree with
that, too. It is, after all, inescapably a facet of being human. Perhaps it becomes more visible here
on the island; maybe we sense the essential need to allow ourselves to embrace all of that which is
a part of us . . . for only in so doing, the healing can begin. ❦

The Truth Deep Within Us

Dedicated to my father, Charles Robert Isleib, 1/31/98

Martha Jean Isleib

un - wavering cer — tain — ty e — ver — y — day The

Truth deep with in us will show us the way! A- men.

2. Watch over us gently, to You we defer.
   In You we seek peace, in faith You assure.
   Each road that we travel, each cloud, soar above
   reminds us that always we find You in love.

3. And if we should ever sink in life's despair,
   We need only look inward, to find You are there.
   When we are ready to go forth once again,
   We'll find You are with us 'round every bend.

4. Watch over our loved ones as now we depart,
   Keep them everpresent deep within our heart.
   With the colors of sunrise, and the winddriven spray
   make us ever mindful that with You love will stay.

The best fig cakes are made on Hatteras Island. Generations of island women pass the recipe along to daughters and friends, and frequently choose from the ripest fruit growing in their own yards. The cake is rich and dense, fragrant and ambrosial, and is carried to community covered-dish events, served at wedding and birthday celebrations, and offered to neighbors in trying times and for funeral suppers. Hatteras children delight in plucking and eating the sweet, sun-warmed figs right from the tree.

Here's what's cookin': Fig cake

Recipe from the kitchen of 325°

1½ c sugar ⎤ cream

3 eggs ⎫
1 c oil ⎪
½ c butter milk ⎬ add + beat
2 c plain flour ⎭ 1 c - 1 pt. figs
1 t salt 1 c nuts
1 t soda ½ c wistey
1 t nutmeg
1 t Allspice Serves:
1 t vanilla

This recipe is from the kitchen
of Edith Stowe Oden

Joyce M. Bornfriend

With family ties to the area, Joyce M. Bornfriend has lived on the Outer
Banks since 1967. Educated at East Carolina University, she has thirty-
five years' experience in public school education. Currently, Joyce is the
education director for the Frisco Native American Museum.

Thirteen Days

By Joyce M. Bornfriend

The weatherman's voice was deep and assured as he pointed to the radar image and announced that a hurricane was brewing in the Atlantic: "We expect this front to pick up speed as it heads toward Cape Hatteras."

How many times had I heard that warning? My mind shifted, and I was transported by a flood of images so vivid I could feel them wash over me.

Suddenly it was 1993, and I was back at Cape Hatteras School, surveying a scene that my eyes recorded yet my mind refused to comprehend. Hurricane Emily had ravaged the island the previous day, and though my husband and I had struggled through the darkening hours to cope with the damage to our home and museum, I had been confident that the school had come through the battering. The school, my school, was the center of our community, a basic part of our community's foundation. The sturdy brick buildings represented more than a facility for learning: they represented safety and stability.

Both of our vehicles were victims of the flood, so I'd had to flag down a car and hitch a ride to the school. My breath came in tight, shallow pockets as I crossed the parking lot. Water slowly dripped from the buses that had been moved to higher ground near the road. The fence surrounding the tennis courts made a jagged line, leaning outward at a 90-degree angle. Twigs, pinecones, tree limbs, and a strange assortment of debris dotted the asphalt and covered the neatly trimmed lawn. To my left, three cars were piled in a tangle, almost touching the exterior wall of the auditorium. The planks used to landscape the area had saved the building from their impact.

The door was ajar, and I stepped into mud and sea grass as I entered the darkened hall. My eyes widened in disbelief. My desk was in the middle of the front entryway! I looked from it to the open doorway with the sign Principal's Office. It had floated through two rooms and come to rest against a chair and a small table. The bottom half of the wood was bleached white from the water's mark, and I touched it gingerly, astonished at the force of water that had pushed massive furniture through locked doors. Student artwork was scattered on the floor or hanging askew along the wall. Dozens of ceiling tiles floated in pools of murky slime, and water dripped from the gaping holes above, making soft, plunking sounds. Lockers hung open, contents spilling bright pools of color on the floor. Rubber molding strips formed a wavy line, buckling out where the glue had dissolved in patches along the wall.

The heat was oppressive, but I barely felt it as the silence closed around me. Moving beyond a jumble of broken furniture, I pushed through a swollen door and made my way to the oldest section of the school. A soft breeze blew through two windows that had blown in, and the sun sparkled on patches of wet tile. Mud, pine straw, and sea grass were everywhere, filling the hall with the organic stench of brine and mold. The odor was almost tangible as I picked my way around broken glass, moving past doors pulled from their hinges, overturned bookcases, and computers scattered on the floor, oozing salty brine, their dark screens stained with sediment. Tree branches and marsh grass lay scattered on counters, and traces of mud could be seen on the wall five feet above the floor. Masses of textbooks and papers were pushed against a closet door, bleeding ink into soft mounds of mush. Bloated files spewed their wet contents, and musty black silt coated almost every surface. All around, the building lay silent.

My footsteps echoed as I slowly made my way through the grimy halls to the media center. It was elevated several feet above the other buildings. Surely it had escaped the devastation.

The acrid smell of salt and mold struck me as I pushed the doors open, but the cheerful room appeared to be in order, furniture placed as we had left it. My initial sigh of relief gave way to a sinking feeling as brackish mush sloshed from the carpet with every step I took. Mud was splashed along the lower edge of the wall, and small chunks of sea grass nestled on the empty bottom shelves. We had shifted books from the lower shelves, saving many of them from the water – but not its effects. A damp coat of mold had already formed on covers and along book spines. Even the walls seemed to be sprouting a gray mass.

I trudged on, finding room after room of mud-stained carpet, splattered walls, salt-drenched equipment, and endless mounds of sodden paper. A frog leaped past my fingers as I bent to pick up a photograph floating in a small puddle of water beneath a broken window. It fell apart in my hand as I tried to make out the face. A teacher's memento. Gone with countless other personal items.

Only the upper floors of the middle school and the gym had escaped the devastating effects of the water's surge. Even there, the smell of salt hung heavy in the air. Just twenty-four hours earlier, the building had been ready for the opening of school. Bright bulletin boards beckoned, learning centers overflowed with supplies, student artwork graced the walls, plants created splashes of color, and floors sparkled from the summer's cleaning and waxing. A new school term awaited – full of promise and excitement.

In the space of a few hours, Hurricane Emily changed everything. School, the place that was supposed to be a safe haven, a refuge for our community, was in shambles.

My mind flashed back to the present. Another hurricane was possibly on the horizon. Heading for Hatteras Island. So much to do. Windows would have to be boarded, cars moved, the boats tied down, everything picked up from the yard, food supplies checked, water drawn . . . the very thought of it all made me tired.

Then my mind took me back to Cape Hatteras School again – this time surrounded by staff members and literally hundreds of volunteers. Temperatures soared as we mucked through the debris and began cleaning the building. A mountain of ruined supplies and equipment grew in front of the school as volunteers formed relays, passing sodden loads down the busy hallways to the waiting tractor. Power hoses sprayed rooms as soon as they were cleared, and borrowed generators were shifted among the work spaces, providing temporary electricity. The quiet of the desolate building was transformed as tentative notes of laughter sounded, and the anguished fears of the first hours were replaced by spirited determination. We *would* rebuild. We would do it quickly so our children could begin the school year and attempt to put thoughts of the hurricane behind them.

The memories crowded one on top of another: the long, agonizing, hot hours of grimy work, the shocked expressions of staff members who had lost their homes, the endless tears and dazed, weary faces seemingly grown old with worry. So many emotions crammed into days that almost stretched us beyond our endurance. But gradually, progress was apparent. Filth disappeared as surfaces were scrubbed, debris shoveled, rooms disinfected, windows repaired, electrical wires replaced, roofs patched, supplies sorted, trees cut, tears wiped, and hands held.

Even then, I smiled as I thought of other moments: the outrageous rumors when a tiny green snake was found among the seaweed on a teacher's desk; the cheerfulness and enthusiasm of National Guardsmen as they hefted huge bookcases and pulled carpet long-stuck to cement floors; the smiles of Methodist men and women as they served meals three times a day; the stream of desperately needed donations, the resourcefulness of staff, the ache of tired muscles, the luxury of a hot bath and an air-conditioned room, the loyalty of friends and the kindness of strangers.

The kindness of strangers. In reality, there were no strangers as we faced what seemed insurmountable tasks. Community members, administrators and staff from other schools came in huge numbers to spend long, grueling hours in back-breaking labor. People who had known the island only as a sunny resort joined with others who had discovered us through the post-hurricane news reports. Their concern and generosity quickly transformed them into treasured friends.

Even optimists scoffed when I promised that school would reopen in two weeks. Our losses were gargantuan. More than fifty computers were gone; more than a thousand books were swollen masses of unreadable mush; textbooks and teaching supplies for one entire building had been bulldozed. Copy machines and audio visual equipment were filled with sea grass. Carpet in the elementary building, media center, administrative offices, and several high school classrooms was beyond salvage; eight air conditioners were totaled, and ten more had suffered extensive damage. Band instruments were submerged in salt water, as was the equipment in the weight room and locker areas. The physical science lab and huge quantities of elementary science equipment were destroyed. Students' desks, lockers, and classroom furniture had already begun rusting from the salt water, and the entire bell and security systems were damaged. The list seemed endless, finally totaling over three million dollars. Open school in two weeks? Impossible.

Yet the impossible happened. Our staff worked eighteen-hour days – seven days a week. National Guard troops, Army workers, U.S. Forestry rangers, county government employees, community volunteers, and "strangers" took on astounding jobs – and got them done! We actually beat the two-week mark. We reopened in thirteen days!

Early on the morning students were to arrive, I walked through the silent halls again, giving the building one last inspection before the momentous day began. My heart swelled with joy at what had been accomplished. Though there was still much work to be done, the results of the past thirteen days were astounding. The lawn was neatly trimmed and free of debris. Buses were already on the road, ready to pick up their precious cargo. The building was again clean and organized. Artwork dotted the white walls, bringing warmth and beauty to the quiet halls. One corner near the high school restrooms had a profusion of green plants, carefully landscaped to hide a section of damaged paint. Lockers stood in straight lines, with only the faint rust stains at the base betraying the recent onslaught. New ceiling tiles made an attractive patchwork design, and fresh paint covered newly sanded doorframes. Donated tables and chairs replaced desks in many classrooms, and though bookcases were not filled, shelves held sufficient materials to get the year underway.

Elementary classrooms had bright splashes of color with carpet squares and room-sized rugs almost hiding the bare cement floors. Dozens of colorful helium balloons had been released in the hallway to draw students' eyes to the ceiling and give the building a festive air. Most important, the staff was prepared to greet the students with an air of victory. We had done more than survive: we had prevailed through hard work, determination, and a shared vision. For a brief and challenging period, we had each stepped beyond the concerns of our individual lives to join forces toward a mutual goal. We had drawn strength from each other and learned one of life's most difficult lessons: even catastrophic loss can be endured and diminished through the love and support of people working together.

The weatherman had moved beyond the impending hurricane to talk about conditions on the West Coast, and my mind shifted back to the present. As I considered the work ahead, I knew that my capable and fantastically resourceful husband would deal with the hurricane warning. We'd batten down the hatches, check our supplies, and we'd do our best to be ready.

The threat of another storm did not change the fact that Hatteras Island is a glorious place to live – for countless reasons, from the serenity and simplicity of the lifestyle to the marvelous people and the stupendous, breathtaking beauty of the island. Hurricanes and hurricane warnings come with the package. From my experience, they are a small price to pay for life in such a magical place. ❦

Mary Anna LaFratta

Mary Anna LaFratta is currently living with someone that loves her
and she, him, in an old cabin with a new addition, surrounded by
trees, far from neighbors, across from the northern boundary of the
Great Smoky Mountain National Park in Eastern Tennessee. Following
her respite on Hatteras Island, Mary Anna returned to university life
and is now an assistant professor teaching at the University of North
Carolina at Asheville.

Identity, Place and Change

Mary Anna LaFratta

The noise awakened me. Instinctively, I looked at the clock. It was early, the red lights on the clock read 4:20. It must be John snoring, I thought. I gently nudged him but the sound coming from him continued. I nudged him again. The sound was not usual. I turned on the light to see him.

John's eyes were open and fixed. I called loudly to his face – there was no movement. I thought he must be in a deep sleep. I shook him and called his name again. He didn't move. Not even the slightest eye movement. I ran to the phone and dialed 911. "My husband isn't breathing . . . I think maybe he is in a deep sleep . . . I'll check him again." It was all so dreamlike. I hung up and quickly went to the bed to check him again to see if I was mistaken.

John's eyes had closed. A drop of saliva moved slowly down his chin from between his lips. I knew this was serious and I had to do something, quickly. Three minutes. Once John had mentioned that without oxygen to the brain, damage would begin within three minutes. My mind was racing. The phone rang. It was the 911 dispatcher calling me back. "He is still not breathing," I said, "1217 Claremont Avenue . . . walk me through CPR."

I pulled John to the floor. His head hit with a thud. I winced and tears flowed down my face. From the corner of my eye I saw the flashing red lights at the edges of the closed blinds. The rescue squad was here. I left John again to open the door.

I led the rescue workers to the bedroom and, giving them space, I stood in the living room staring out the window through the blinds, remembering the last time I saw the same flashing lights when a neighbor had died. I prayed for John to live.

Something was very wrong here. The workers had been in the room with John for a long time, much longer than three minutes. I must have called my mother at some point, though I don't remember, but she, my sister and a friend, Dee, arrived at the house. Dee had worked with John on a county volunteer rescue squad. I asked her to go into the bedroom and to make sure the squad workers were doing everything they could.

Eventually, everyone emerged from the room. John was on a gurney with an apparatus on his face. He was loaded into the rescue squad vehicle. The rest of us followed to the hospital. I asked Dee, "What do you think, will John live? Tell me the truth." She responded, "Things do not look good."

Dee went into a back room with the emergency room doctor. Minutes passed. I paced the hall and watched as the rest of my brothers and sisters filed into the hospital hallway. I knew John was dead. In an instant he left me and my life was different.

I regretted that I had moved outside of John's field of view when his eyes were still open, not looking deep into his eyes, not holding him tight, and saying "I love you." I regret not knowing how to start him breathing again. I am deeply, deeply saddened beyond what words can describe.

John was a cardiac technician working in an emergency room for a large hospital, and a volunteer with a local rescue squad. He was forty-two years old, handsome, funny and my best friend. We were married for ten years. Now I was alone with our dog, Barney, a large, eleven-year-old black and white mixed breed. We both missed John.

I later learned that the noise I thought was snoring was the last air leaving John's lungs, an involuntary action. By the time this occurs the brain stem is already dead, so I was told.

There was an autopsy and the doctors declared that John had died of respiratory failure; they speculated on the causes. His lungs had been moderately full of fluid and he had a mild viral pneumonia.

One of the doctors that accompanied me to the meeting to hear the autopsy report had worked with John in the ER. She said that possibly the virus had interrupted the electrical charges to his heart and that caused it to slowly come to a stop.

I had John's body cremated, a decision that had to be made just hours after his passing. Although John had previously talked of not having a church service of any kind, I overrode this request – so many of his friends and family required closure. There was a memorial service and three hundred people attended. The organist, a treasured friend of John's, opened the event by playing *Let It Be*, written by The Beatles, as the members of the volunteer rescue squad marched down the center church aisle dressed in uniform with black ribbons tied on the upper portion of their left arms.

I took my accumulated sick leave from work and stayed inside my house allowing things to sink in. All the others had returned to their lives, while the grieving process for me was settling in like a heavy stone on my heart. I ached all over. The house was so quiet. My dog was my only companion. No one called on me.

After weeks of isolation, Barney and I headed to West Virginia, escorted by my brother. I had wanted to see friends and to revisit a place that John and I held dear. Later, still requiring someone to guide us, a good friend from Maine flew down to Virginia and escorted Barney and me on a drive back to Maine. The escort was my girlfriend's husband. I had wanted to spend time with them both and to get out of the house, but for whatever reason, was afraid to venture anywhere alone. I am not sure why; looking back, it seemed to be a side effect of losing my best friend, my life partner and my identity that had evolved over my years with him.

Eventually, Barney and I traveled alone. We went to Frisco, on the southern end of Hatteras Island. It was April, sunny and warm. We had been invited by a buddy of John's to stay at his house in the upstairs room for as long as we needed. And we did. Barney settled in downstairs with two other large dogs and I was given a space of my own, a small quaint room in what fondly was referred to as the attic.

I made the space comfortable. I moved in plants, hung lace curtains and brought down from Virginia enough things – clothes, books, photographs – so the room felt secure. The room and the house grew to be my refuge, and John's friend grew to be like a brother. We enjoyed each other's company, we shared dinners together and trips to the beach with now three very large black dogs.

It was during the months between April and August in 1997, that I often contemplated in which direction to go – back to Virginia, out West to start a new life, or to take a long walk into the ocean. Since I had no answers, I decided to stay and in September I rented my own place. It was in a beautiful location, down a sandy road surrounded by trees, hidden from neighboring houses, perched high overlooking the Pamlico Sound. It was a place for me to endure the first winter without John, and to live through his birthday, my birthday, Christmas, New Year's Day, the day of his death, and our wedding anniversary.

I took a leave of absence from my job in Virginia as a university professor. I picked up part-time work at the local bookstore, a perfect job for me. The building was quaint and packed with interesting things, books, notes, candles, and a variety of related objects. I enjoyed the space. It was there that I met many wonderful women, others that for various reasons came to live on the island and chose to also work at a bookstore. It was a unique place to work. Although I was a sales clerk, the types of customers were different, unlike those you'd find frequenting the typical tourist gift shop searching for trinkets and T-shirts.

The wage was low and the average rent for a house, not a trailer, was around six hundred dollars a month, plus utilities. The cost of living on the island was equal to that of the city where I lived and I suspect, equal to that of other large cities in the South. I also picked up a few freelance assignments writing for the island's monthly paper. Although I had written nothing up to this point in my life beyond university memos, curriculum proposals and student project descriptions, the editor of the paper was kind to me. She passed on encouragement and gave me pointers. However, I suspected that she and the readers were not inspired by my writings. Discouraged by my lack of skill and the excruciating low rate of pay, I stopped writing for the paper after several seasons.

On inspiration, one of those women that had worked at the bookstore with me sent me an advertisement she saw in the back of *Writers' Digest*, a trade journal. The ad was seeking a technical writer for a textbook publishing company. I responded and sent all of the required materials. Months later, I received a call from them offering me a job to write several units for their distance learning course in art that was offered to adults. I accepted and received a long-term (nearly two years) contract to write from my home on the island.

After living on the island for more than a year, I made the decision to break all ties with my previous life. I quit my job at the university and sold my house in Virginia. I moved what I could to the island and stored the rest at my mother's house and in my sister's attic. It is interesting to me that for years I had wanted to leave the university and to live outside of Virginia, and it took an event so devastating to make it happen.

For several years I had a ritual of dispersing John's ashes into the ocean's waters on his birthday. I waited for the time when the tide was traveling back out into itself. I'd go to a quiet, less frequently visited section of beach in Frisco. I would draw a heart with our initials inside and sprinkle ashes into its center and watch the water take them away. Sometimes I'd include his birthday and death day and watch the words, and his remnants, disappear. Time moves on. It is such a constant.

I made an effort to integrate myself into the community and soon began to see the island and its lifestyle from a perspective different from that of a passer-by.

It is a place of extremes, calm and rough waters, heat, wind, rain and hurricanes. It is a place where abundant nature and commercial decadence fight to exist side by side. It is a place of rich and poor, of serfs and lords. It is a place of severe disconnection between the land and water and the greedy self-interests of a population of people that, like the rest of the United States, are consumers.

I watched out my window during Hurricane Dennis as inadequate septic tanks overflowed and sewage spread across yards. The dirty water covered the vegetable garden beds I had tended and nurtured for months. These waters mixed with stream waters that connected to the sound and ocean. Still I wonder if there exists regular septic inspections and how developers obtain approvals for chlorinated swimming pools adjacent to the ocean, and houses outfitted with numerous bathrooms, complete with Jacuzzis and hot tubs. I wonder how they manage to get approval to fill in wetlands and why the drinking water is discolored and tastes so bad.

These things are not unique to Hatteras Island. It seems commonplace over the entire planet. It is just that these physical realities are at odds with a place that has such ability for spiritual renewal. It is nature that provides this healing and it is what drew many to the island in the first place.

For nearly four years I made Frisco my home and the southern section of Hatteras Island and Ocracoke Island my regular habitat. I was beginning to live on money I had in savings on a regular basis and it was nearly impossible to make enough to sustain living in the house, to maintain my car, and to pay my bills. It became more difficult for me to grow further in the fields of interest that were always cultivated at the university. I began to look beyond this place that sits miles from the mainland as the need to explore another place grew prevalent. With much reluctance, I left. I moved away thinking that I needed more natural space in which to roam and to make new discoveries.

As of this writing it has been just over two years since I left behind the place that renewed my soul and provided me with many friends. Some of those friends have also moved on. John's friend who had allowed me to stay in his house in Frisco, my new brother, is now living in Great Britain. Three friends have died from cancer, leaving behind their families to renew themselves on the island. One friend has committed to regularly corresponding with me and developing our evolving friendship. For all of these things I am grateful. ❧

For though they may be parted there is still a chance that they will see,
there will be an answer, let it be. – The Beatles

Patricia J. Moore

Patricia J. Moore retired to Hatteras Island in 1991. After
receiving a masters degree in education, she was a secondary
teacher in Arkansas, Ohio, Missouri and Maryland, the many
moves brought on by her husband's transfers in his government
job. When she isn't birding, she enjoys reading, sewing, working
crossword puzzles, and researching her family's genealogy. She is
affiliated with bird clubs on the state level in North Carolina,
Maryland and Arkansas, and with the American Birding
Association and National Audubon Society.

Passion on the Wing

Patricia J. Moore

Life is good on Hatteras Island, a mighty fine destination for people who pursue interests in outdoor activities. My husband, Neal, and I began an odyssey that moved us from Middle America to a mid-Atlantic state from which we visited here as tourists for fishing and birding. We made the drive at least twice a year for twenty-five years and ended up moving here. We are the envy of friends we left behind who have to drive five to ten hours to reach this setting of ocean, beach, sound, sand dune, salt marsh, sedge, and maritime forest. We treasure the fragile environment and untouched places that lend so much to the reasons that brought us here.

Red-breasted Nuthatches, wintertime visitors, feed along tree branches while making their little yank-yank call.

There is so much to do. I came here to watch birds. Neal came to fish, but golf has shouldered that aside, and birding has edged its way into his life. For me, most of my adult life has been spent observing and listening to birds. It is such an obsession that I hear birdsong when I should be paying mind to other things. I notice birds when others are unaware of creatures on the wing. I round out my interest by doing pen-and-ink illustrations of birds, with a little calligraphy on the side.

On our first trip here, I was so "unacquainted" with the ocean that I didn't know about Sanderlings. They were just those amusing little birds on the shore that ran in and out with the tide, never getting their feet wet. The eight kinds of gulls all looked alike at first, but after ten years of repetition, first as a student, then as "teacher," I've learned to identify most of the species in their various plumages. I was entranced with The Point and its many faces, sometimes calm, sometimes very rough and stormy. I was fascinated by all the seabirds that I'd never seen before: the Northern Gannets that sometimes wheeled about in the hundreds, the Double-crested Cormorants that winter in the thousands, the

straight-line flights of the various scoters – new sea ducks for me. New, too, were the Ruddy Turnstones, the Willets and Whimbrels. These birds are often seen when the weather is not at its best.

Here one is closer to the weather than in parts of the country less affected by unusual forecasts. We have lived in places that were tornado- and flood-prone, places where ice storms broke trees, and where snow closed a county for several days, but none of those places were as weather-conscious as Hatteras Island. We moved here knowing that hurricanes and nor'easters would be a part of our lives, so we built a sturdy house.

Ruby-throated Hummingbirds were one of the biggest surprises when we moved here. They visit feeders on Hatteras Island the year around!

The upside of unpredictable weather is the wealth of birds that are often blown in by a storm, for a most abundant array of species can appear. We birders hurry to the places on the beaches and in the vegetated areas where the bewildered birds are known to put down to rest and forage for food.

All seasons bring something new. We are glad when spring comes, but then it is good to see the birds of summer. We can hardly wait for summer to end because the change brings fall migration when the element of surprise is never better than finding birds that get off course during their trips south. But then winter is extremely exciting because of the variety and abundance of seabirds, waterfowl, songbirds, and occasional strays – birds that get "lost" during migration and end up here rather than in their proper destination.

Many of those wanderers stop by the Cape Point area, where we have seen Western Grebe, Swallow-tailed Kite, Sabine's Gull, Common Murre, Eurasian Widgeon, Scissor-tailed Flycatcher, Sooty Tern and Greater Shearwater, all exceptional birds for this location.

We are the envy of our inland friends who do not have our regular "canal birds": Green Heron, Black Skimmer, various gulls, wintering ducks and grebes, and an occasional Common Loon. We enjoy the Carolina Wren that starts our winter mornings and the nocturnal Chuck-will's-widow that calls through summer nights.

Yes, along with the birds, Hatteras Island is the proper destination for us. We are happy to be here as we grow older because we are staying active by volunteering and enjoying adventures with all ages. As volunteers, a standard pursuit for many of the island's retirees, we help with birdwalks for both the National Park Service and Fish and Wildlife Service. We are involved with an annual festival, Wings over Water, that celebrates the outdoor wonders of coastal North Carolina. Our membership in Cape Hatteras Bird Club helps keep us busy. Founded in the late 1980s, the club has been the perfect means of getting to know other birders by participation in meetings and trips afield.

Through our birding and Neal's golfing and fishing, we have made so many enduring friend-ships that we feel that we are the luckiest people around. Yes, life is good on Hatteras Island. 🐦

Belted Kingfishers, island residents, can be found on wires and posts near the island's canals and ponds.

The Peregrine Falcon, left, another wintering species, can be found perched among the dunes at Cape Point. This swift and powerful raptor preys upon other birds that winter in the area.

Pat Gaved Taylor

In her career as an educator in computer technology, Pat Gaved Taylor traveled extensively throughout the world. She and her family vacationed at her beach cottage in Avon for many years, and she eventually moved to Frisco in 1995 and established the Hatteras Island Pet Resort. Pat is the author of two collections of short stories, "The Legend of the Tooth Fairy" and "A Fisherman's Luck," and has written an account of the trials and tribulations of building an island boarding facility, "A Barrier Island Kennel."

The Pines of Hatteras

Pat Gaved Taylor

Did you know that trees can speak? Not, of course, in the way you or I do but they do have their own voices and if you listen awhile in the island woods you will begin to hear them.

The tall, slender pine trees whisper softly in their upper branches when the breeze is gentle. During a nor'easter their needles can make fearful, angry hissing noises and their branches groan as though they resent the fierce, cold wind. The live oaks, their broad solid trunks anchoring them in the sandy soil, speak more softly through their small, evergreen leaves. The palmettos are perhaps the noisiest, like a bunch of gossips, with the constant clacking of their fan-like fronds. The yaupon and cedars only sigh quietly unless there is a gale and then they can produce a peculiar, high-pitched sound, almost as though they are singing. Sometimes a delicate, feathery tree that in early summer has deep orange flowers, may join in as it rattles its dry seeds in their pods (which gives it the name of Rattlebox), almost like the accompaniment in a Mexican mariachi band.

Every other tree, bush and plant on the Outer Banks has its own soft voice too, but this story is really about the pine trees.

I must explain first about the pines of Hatteras Island and why they are here. Many years ago, at the beginning of the twentieth century, some of the islanders kept cattle that they allowed to run free all over the island. In a way the cattle were destructive because they ate all the new shoots of the live oaks that are native trees, but didn't care for the resinous taste of young pines. Because of this, the whole nature of the original maritime forest changed. The pine trees flourished and soon formed dense forests that choked out or stunted most of the live oaks and the tall canopies of pine needles kept the sunlight from the bushes on the ground below them. So, for many years the maritime forest was formed mainly of pine trees, with just a few native trees and bushes struggling to survive.

Then, on the last day of August 1993, a hurricane called Emily, that had been building and gaining power in the South Atlantic, roared in and made landfall on Hatteras Island.

It was during the peak season for visitors and almost every beach cottage was occupied. Nevertheless, the rental companies went to each cottage and told the renters that they must leave the island. A few people, thinking it would be "fun" to sit out a hurricane, refused to leave, but when the police and rescue services came by and politely insisted, telling them that they could be without water, telephones or electricity and possibly, if the ocean washed out the roads, be unable to leave for several days, even the most reckless and irresponsible visitors understood and evacuated. It was just as well, because Emily devastated the island.

High winds twisted beach cottages almost off their pilings, the waters of the sound were driven by the winds into a seven-foot tide that, having nowhere else to go, broke out across the island to escape to the ocean. The tide came so quickly that many of the residents in the villages lost everything as their houses were inundated by water. Some people did not even have insurance to pay for the damage. The winds reached around one hundred and thirty miles an hour and if you don't believe how dangerous that is, you should have seen my own beach cottage afterwards. Three of my bedrooms were gutted; windows were blown in, beds overturned, pictures and mirrors vaporized, and doors and their wood frames blown violently into the corridor. In spite of the pilings being sunk six feet into the ground, the whole house was leaning over almost two feet from vertical and the crosspieces bracing the pilings were either bowed or broken. All the outside steps were skewed and the top deck railing was disconnected and waving several feet out from the deck floor.

This only gives you an idea of what Emily did to the island.

Yet, some good may have come out of even such a disaster. For the invading pine trees that had taken over the maritime woods were damaged not once but twice. Hundreds were snapped in half by the random tornados spawned by the hurricane and most of the rest were so twisted and stressed by the winds that they fell prey to an insect called the pine beetle. This creature prefers the bark of dead pines but there were so many of these and the beetles multiplied so rapidly that they began to invade those pines that were still alive (though only barely).

You could walk up to the trunk of a pine, see the quarter-inch holes in its bark and know it was doomed, for there is no spray or other treatment that can save these trees once they are infested. Nor does anyone particularly want to save them. The pines are shallow-rooted, unlike the live oaks, and frequently blow down in regular storms to block the highway and people's driveways, sever electric lines and land on roofs of houses. So they are not loved – or even admired – by the islanders.

Next time you drive down to the southern part of the island that is about three miles past the lighthouse, you can see the brown-needled or bare pines standing stark and dead in Buxton Woods (or Trent Woods, if you prefer the original name).

Don't mourn them, for they had their day and were really nothing but invaders. Instead, look at how the formerly stunted live oaks have begun to flourish, as well as the cattails, native grasses, vines and flowers. If you take the time to look closer, you will also see the deer, birds, butterflies, moths, tree frogs and other original inhabitants who once more have a congenial environment.

There are still plenty of majestic, towering pines in the woods, but they no longer threaten to take over the maritime forest that is rare enough in this country and is at last recovering its full beauty. The deer and other creatures, birds and insects are grateful, and we should be too. Hurricane Emily was bad for the island, but in years to come, the bad effects may be somewhat balanced by what she did that was good. 🦑

The Legend of the Tooth Tree

Pat Gaved Taylor

All over the Outer Banks you can find a deciduous tree not much larger than a tall bush. In summer it has pale green leaves. These leaves are long and slender, fanning out from their central stems. In winter you would hardly notice the tree's low, rounded silhouette of bare grey branches, unless there is the rare ice storm and the sound freezes. Then the tree may be coated with ice and sparkling in the sun. If you look carefully you will see several of them on the dune side between Avon and Buxton.

Visitors do not stop to admire the Tooth Tree because it is really rather ordinary-looking, just another bush like the yaupon. Most people driving by never even notice it. But for the small birds of Hatteras Island, it is very special.

Long, long ago the branches of the Tooth Tree were smooth. Yet today you may easily recognize it by the large thorns that cover every twig and branch from the trunk up to very tip of its branches. So how did the Tooth Tree get its thorns? Listen and I'll tell you.

Everyone knows about the Tooth Fairy, who, when you lost a baby tooth and put it under your pillow, would leave a dime or a quarter in its place. But have you ever wondered what the Tooth Fairy does with those tiny, white teeth?

Well, one day the Tooth Fairy was traveling down Hatteras Island taking care of all the little children who had lost their baby teeth and were putting them under their pillows. She stopped to rest for a while on a sand dune and was gazing out at the ocean when a fledgling bird fluttered onto a yaupon bush nearby. The young bird, whose name was Wheek-wheek, looked at the Tooth Fairy, who is slender and beautiful and very, very tiny – not much taller than a blade of grass – and the little bird was not afraid. In fact, he decided he would sing her a song.

Wheek-wheek fluffed his feathers, flapped his wings, raised his beak and tried to sing. But he was only a fledgling and all he could produce from his pulsing little throat were a few chirrups and squeaks. He was embarrassed and was about to fly away when the Tooth Fairy spoke to him.

"That was charming," she said. She was being quite truthful, for if Wheek-wheek's song had been off-key (and he never would be much of a singer, even when he grew up) she appreciated that he had tried. "In return for your song," she went on, "I would like to do something for you but I don't know what little birds like."

"Oh berries and seeds and things," said Wheek-wheek shyly, "but please don't bother as I can gather those for myself."

"There must be something else," the Tooth Fairy insisted.

Wheek-wheek cocked his head to one side and gazed for a moment, hesitated and then said, "Well, there is something I have been thinking about, but it's silly really because I'm only a bird…"

"Go on," said the Tooth Fairy. "It won't do any harm to tell me and perhaps I can find a way to help."

"All right," said Wheek-wheek, with a little more confidence. "It's like this. Little birds like me only have beaks." Then he stopped and pretended to preen his wing feathers.

"But of course you do," the Tooth Fairy replied. "And very pretty they are too," she added, for Wheek-wheek's beak was a soft yellow and contrasted beautifully with his pale gray and chocolate-brown plumage.

"That's the trouble," Wheek-wheek said, all in a rush before he lost his courage. "You see, we don't have any teeth! I mean, we don't need them but it would be nice if…"

"If what?" the Tooth Fairy prompted him.

Wheek-wheek stretched his neck upwards, fluffed his new feathers and shifted his feet on the yaupon branch. Then he settled himself again. "Baby birds don't get anything under their pillows," he finally blurted out. Then he hurriedly preened his feathers again.

"Ah, now I understand," the Tooth Fairy said gently, and she did. Because of course her job was to give human children a dime or a quarter for their baby teeth, which made them happy, but the little birds got nothing. "Let me think about this," she told Wheek-wheek. "Where do you live?"

"In that big live oak, next to the sound," Wheek-wheek replied. "It's not very safe because of the hawks, you know, but this year we have been lucky and no one has been taken…away."

"Don't worry, I'll be back," the Tooth Fairy told him sympathetically. "Until then, be careful and stay close to your home." She rose from the sand, spread her delicate gossamer wings (because fairies are really very like butterflies) and was borne away on the ocean breeze.

"Oh well, I tried," Wheek-wheek said to himself. "And besides, I shouldn't have asked for anything in return for my song. That really wasn't polite." Then he fluttered his newly fledged wing feathers, of which he was very proud, and flew back to his parents' nest.

Some time passed and Wheek-wheek was busy practicing his flying, which got better and better, and his singing, which stayed much the same no matter how hard he tried. In fact, his brothers and sisters in the nest finally convinced him he would never be a songbird and should limit his chirps to simple bird talk.

The Tooth Fairy was busy too, but she did not forget her conversation with the little bird and she worried at the problem until one day the answer came to her. "Of course!" she exclaimed to herself. "Little birds do not need money, for how would they spend it? But I shall do something much better for them." The next time she visited Hatteras to take care of the young children who had put their baby teeth under their pillows, she alighted on the live oak tree where Wheek-wheek had his home.

The sun had set over the sound but the sky still held the glorious rose-pinks and golds and purples, and the waves breaking on the sands reflected those colors in turquoise and copper and silver. Wheek-wheek and his family were just settling down in their nest, ready to put their heads under their wings and go to sleep when the Tooth Fairy arrived.

"Don't let me disturb you," she said to Wheek-wheek and his parents and brothers and sisters, "but I have some news that you may want to pass on to the other small birds on the island." Then she proceeded to tell them.

The next morning Wheek-wheek and his family rose from their nest, sang their sunrise-greeting song and then flew off to see if what the Tooth Fairy had told them was true. To their joy it was. Everywhere, all over the island, the low-growing bushes with their smooth branches that had seemed so ordinary, and had merely been places to rest when flying from one place to another, had sprouted thorns! And what thorns! Twice as long and wide as the claws of the most ferocious cat, they clothed the trees from the ground up to the topmost branches.

Just as the Tooth Fairy had promised, she had created a refuge where they could nest and always be safe. No cat or snake or hawk or human could disturb them, for the thorns were too fierce. The birds would always be protected as long as they built their homes in the Tooth Tree. The little bird, Wheek-wheek, and his family and all the other small birds were very happy.

So now you know what the Tooth Fairy does with the children's baby teeth that she takes from under their pillows. She uses them to make thorns on the Tooth Tree to protect the little birds.

And so it has been ever since. 🦷

Barbara Satterthwaite-Hebenstreit

Barbara Satterthwaite-Hebenstreit was born in Newtown, Bucks
County, Pennsylvania, where the highlight of her childhood was
romping in the woods and playing baseball with the boys in the
fields around her home (using manure chips for bases). She attended
a one-room school for five years. Barbara is the office manager for
"The Island Breeze" newspaper, and says if she had her life to live
over, she wouldn't change a thing.

Hooked on Surf-fishing

Barbara Satterthwaite-Hebenstreit

What brought me to Hatteras Island? The surf-fishing and beautiful beaches.

In the early '70s, my parents read an article about Cape Hatteras in *National Geographic* and during a trip driving back from Florida, stopped in Buxton for a few days. From then on they were hooked on Hatteras Island and spent two months (spring and fall) out of the year surf-fishing on Hatteras Island and staying at the Tower Circle Motel with Jack Gray. In 1981 my parents were ready to consummate a deal on purchasing a home and moving to this area from Newtown, Bucks County, Pennsylvania but that all changed when my father had a stroke while vacationing here and passed away a year later.

In the mid '70s, my parents had talked me into coming down to see their place called Paradise. I did and was hooked on surf-fishing from the day I arrived, just as they were. My father taught me how to cast with a big surf rod and before leaving, I bought myself a surf rod and reel from Kitty Lourie in Buxton.

For the next ten to twelve years I spent four weeks out of the year surf-fishing on Hatteras Island. In between, I met my husband up north and introduced him to Hatteras – here again, another one hooked on Hatteras and surf-fishing.

On our last trip to Hatteras, we became serious and bought a lot and had a home built in Frisco. We both sold our own respective businesses in Philadelphia – Jack, a commercial art business (which he had for over thirty years), and myself, a typesetting business I had operated for fifteen years. We sold our home in Lindenwold, New Jersey and moved into our home in Frisco in November 1989, with both of us unemployed. Within two weeks of moving we experienced a two-day blizzard. We had no heat and our pipes froze, but this did not keep us from staying. We discovered what a great community of people live here and how everyone looks out for one another. Our electric co-op worked beyond the call of duty to get power restored over the Christmas holiday.

By the following spring I had found two jobs – one cleaning rooms at a major motel and the other working as a waitress at a local restaurant. Within a year or so I was holding down three jobs, the third one with a local monthly newspaper. However, working so much did not keep me from surf-fishing every chance I could get. I eventually wore out my Jeep Laredo and bought myself a Ford F150 truck. My husband, although retired, continued to keep himself busy as an artist painting watercolors and displaying them in local art galleries on consignment.

Before long, I found myself fishing in all of the surf-fishing tournaments here. There are four of 'em. The Ocracoke Tournament takes place the first week in May. The Hatteras Village Civic Association holds its own surf-fishing tournament, usually the second or third week in September. In October, we travel up to Nags Head for that tournament, which takes place the first week of the month. The most prestigious and largest surf-fishing tournament on the Atlantic coast takes place the first week in November and is run by the Cape Hatteras Anglers Club, of which I am a member.

For me, it has become wonderfully satisfying to fish in all of these tournaments. It's not the winning of these tournaments to which I look forward, but more the camaraderie I have come to enjoy over the years with all of the participants as well as my team members. I fish on an all-women's team and a few years ago, we found a sponsor for our team, Team Daiwa. Our team name is the Island Girls and not one of us is under fifty! Most of the women on our team are retired except for myself and one other woman who manages a fishing pier with her husband in Frisco.

Fishing in these surf-fishing tournaments is not an easy task. The day before the tournament, the team captain registers his/her team and draws for four positions out of a hat. The numbers drawn are where the team is expected to fish the following two days. Teams fish four sessions in four different areas on the beach over a two-day period – a.m. (usually from 7 – 10) and p.m. (1:30 – 4:30). That is six hours of fishing a day, rain, wind or shine. When fishing on a team, each member tries fishing with a different type of bait and rig. Also, a few members will cast out far, while the others throw in close, just to find out where the fish are and what kind of meal the fish prefer that day. For example, a sea mullet might prefer a bloodworm or cut bait in the morning and by the afternoon may want to eat a sand flea or a strip of squid.

The toughest team fishing I've ever experienced was a few years ago in Ocracoke fishing for the Cape Hatteras Anglers Club. The winds were blowing around twenty-five to thirty miles an hour during our first session in the morning and the weather was predicted only to get worse! By day number two, the wind was blowing a steady fifty miles per hour in our last session – not much fun, especially when the fish weren't biting. One woman fished the entire tournament by herself, as her team never showed up for the tournament. She received a special award for sticking it out and fishing nonstop by herself in the horrible weather during the entire tournament.

My greatest fishing achievement occurred thirteen years ago fishing for black drum on a charter boat out of Cape Charles, Virginia. I was fishing with five men and hooked into a black drum with only twenty-pound test line using an Ugly Stick. One and one-half hours later, I landed a seventy-two-pound black drum – a Virginia citation!

Another exciting feat was fishing with Spurgeon Stowe out of Hatteras on the Miss Hatteras headboat. I knew I was in trouble when a harness was strapped to me (while standing up – no fighting chair) with a large rod and reel. The first mate put a large fish on my hook and floated my line off the stern of the boat. Within seconds I had a large blue fin tuna on my line and thirty to forty minutes later landed and released a three hundred- to three hundred and fifty-pound tuna. Wow! When not tuna fishing that day, in between we were all bottom fishing and bringing in ten- to twelve-pound bluefish.

Surf-fishing is like a disease. You just can't get enough of it – the anticipation of that first bite (while holding your surf rod) and then pulling back and hooking and reeling in a fish. Another aspect I find enjoyable about surf-fishing is teaching others how to fish, especially if they show an interest in it. It is such a thrill to see someone bring in his or her first fish and get hooked on the sport as I did years ago.

My mother passed away five years after my father died. I still miss them very much, but I feel their presence, and know they are watching over me every day I am on the beach surf-fishing.

Between working a great deal and taking care of our home, I don't fish as much now as I did when I first moved here. I have no regrets over moving to this beautiful island thirteen years ago. At times I wish I had made the move sooner. The ocean air kind of gets in your blood and stays there, along with that exciting obsession for catching fish! 🐟

Natalie Perry

Natalie Perry is a sixth-generation Hatteras Islander, who grew up on the island and was graduated from the University of North Carolina at Wilmington. After several years of living and working off-island, she returned to work in the family business, Frisco Rod & Gun and Frisco Market. She is a board member of the Outer Banks Preservation Association, president of the Hatteras Island Genealogical and Historical Society, and a member of the Hatteras Island First Flight committee.

Reunion

Natalie Perry

Last summer I sat at a table in the Anglers Club in Buxton and realized that an entire branch of my family tree surrounded me in the room. We had gathered for a reunion of the Barnett family, a rare occurrence since many of us are now scattered about the country. Members of our family have lived on Cape Hatteras for six generations or more. We have Lifesaving Station Surfmen, Lighthouse Keepers and Coast Guardsmen in our family history. We are proud of the accomplishments of the men of our family. Their service to the island and to our country is recorded in photographs and official documents. The stories of our women are just as important to us, but are only shared in personal collections of photographs and from stories passed down through the years. That reunion weekend allowed our older relatives to reminisce and our younger family members to learn a little about the past.

My great-grandmother Martha and great-grandfather Thomas had seven daughters and four sons: Alivia, Helen, Thomas, Eileen, Iris, Letitia, Chiswell, Grace, my grandmother Georgia, David and Ward. Many people my age (I am 28 years old) think of that as an extremely large family, but it was more common then. The oldest child was born in 1913 and the youngest was born in 1931. The children grew up here on the island and over the years many of them moved away for various reasons. They worked, married, and raised families all over the country. That reunion brought five of these siblings, their families and the families of those siblings who have passed on here to the island for a weekend of catching up with everyone.

My grandmother Georgia and great-aunt Iris live here on Cape Hatteras. Great-aunt Grace and great-uncle Chiswell traveled a long way to join us. My great-uncle Ward, who died October 2002, lived here and was at our reunion that summer. Many of my cousins live here, but others had to travel great distances. I can sympathize with their long drives because I once lived off-island also. It was always so wonderful to get a chance to come back home. Vacations and visits never seemed to last long enough to see everyone I wanted to see. It seemed that just when I would unwind enough to fall back into the pace of the island, it would be time to go back to the city again.

I grew up here on the island surrounded by family and friends. When I went away to college in Wilmington, North Carolina I was terribly homesick at first. I know I annoyed my very understanding roommate, Allison, talking about Cape Hatteras all day. In time, as I met people and got into the routine of my classes and extra-curricular activities, I did not pine for home as much, but I still made the drive to Hatteras every chance I got. It was an uplifting feeling to crest the rise of the Oregon Inlet Bridge and see the narrow expanse of the island before me. I came home every summer and worked for my parents at Frisco Shopping Center and for my friend, Gee Gee Rosell, at Buxton Village Books.

When I graduated from college I came back for one last summer at home before I left for a job in Louisiana. That September, just before I was planning to leave, I remember sitting on the porch of the bookstore with Gee Gee. The sky was brilliant blue above us and the air was warm, but not heavy. We were drinking coffee ice cream milk shakes from the Cool Wave in Buxton and discussing a batch of books that had just arrived at the store that day. It hit me suddenly. I was leaving Cape Hatteras and all the people and places I cared about for an unknown city that was far away from here. I would not be able to return for holidays and long weekends at home like I did when I was at college. What was I thinking? What was I doing? I was supposed to leave the next week and who knew when I would be back? At that point I had already leased an apartment and was all packed to leave. If I backed out now it would look as if I were a coward to not go out in the real world and at least see what it was like. So I left.

I learned a lot in the years I was gone. I found out about office politics. I learned how to drive on interstates that looked just as wide as they were long. I discovered how to navigate airports to make a connecting flight on time. But, after a year in Baton Rouge and a transfer to Tampa, Florida where I spent two more years, I had had enough of the outside world and was ready to return to Cape Hatteras. The excitement of moving to new places had worn thin. I was no longer challenged by my job at the company where I was working. I was frustrated by the daily traffic jams and the constant noise of the city. I felt closed in by my small, yet expensive, apartment. As I lay in bed, instead of hearing the soft rush of the ocean washing against the sand, I would be awakened by the clamor and woo-woo of speeding trains that passed my apartment throughout the night. On a positive note, I did make many wonderful friends in both cities. They filled in as my surrogate family. I joined their families for Thanksgiving and Easter. I would spend my week-ends exploring the places I had moved to with those friends as tour guides. But, after three years of being away, I was ready to come back to Hatteras.

On the fourteen-hour drive home that December, I began to worry about how things might have changed. I wondered if I would fit back into the community. Doubts followed me all the way up I-95. Would I like working at my parent's store again? Would I miss the social life to which I had become accustomed? Would I ever date again? Being alone in a car on a long drive can make a person crazy. So, before I had a panic attack, I started to think about all the good things that I would be returning to when I got back. The best thing would be to have my family near me again. I thought about being able to walk on the beach with my mother and the hunting trips in the sound with my father. I looked forward to my brother Kyle's homecoming from college for Christmas break.

I began to think about my grandmother and my great–aunts on that drive home and all the places they had lived. When they decided to come home, either for a visit or to live as islanders again, they fit back into the community. They took up friendships where they left off and rejoined the family circles that they had been absent from while they were gone. You see, they all knew something I didn't. They knew that when you are an island kid, the island would always be home for you.

When I made it to my front door in Buxton that night I was so happy to be home. The family dog, Rip, was so excited to see me he knocked me flat over on the porch. I was back and I was happy to be here. Now, two years later, I am firmly entrenched in my community. I go to the high school ball games and yell for the kids. I am involved in two volunteer organizations, one to protect our island's future and one to preserve our island's past. I am learning lots of things about my family's store that never caught my attention in the past. I have found my old friends and made a few new ones.

While I was away I realized that on our island the community already exists. A person only has to come home again and fit right back like a missing puzzle piece. You go to the grocery store and you know most of the other people shopping around you. At the bank you know the teller's name, and not because it is pinned to his or her shirt or is on a plaque on the desk. These people are part of your village.

In the "real world" you have to go out into the gridwork of the city and try to find people with whom you connect. You look for people with similar interests or meet people who are related to you by work and try to build a community for yourself. What you end up with is usually a group made up of unmatched people that never seem to fit together at a party or gathering. If you work really hard you can do it. I think I prefer our long-standing, salt-steeped bond that has formed from generations of families living on this island together. I am happy to be home among these families again.

On the last day of our Barnett family reunion we had a big picnic on the grounds of the home where those eleven brothers and sisters grew up. Before everyone left and headed back to their respective homes, we all gathered for pictures on the porch of the old house. My grandmother and her brothers and sisters sat for a picture, and then just my grandmother and her sisters sat to have their pictures taken together. As the three women posed for the photograph, I recalled my thoughts on that drive home two years ago. My reunion with Cape Hatteras was the best choice I could have made. My reunion with my family last summer reminds me why I made it. ❦

Bettie Currie

Bettie Currie was born and reared in Austin, Texas and after schooling, lived in Richmond, Virginia, Philadelphia, Pennsylvania and Washington, D.C. She moved to Frisco with her partner, Mary Talley, in 1977, aiming to focus on their home, Sea Note, and to live co-creatively with all life around them. Bettie was president of the Frisco Civic League and her interests include a love for music and art. She currently makes her home in Virginia Beach, Virginia.

Two Maidens' Voyage

Bettie Currie

We might have been a set for a beer commercial – sitting there in our fifteen-foot boat, exhausted, pleased and toasting each other with a single can of once-cold beer! It was the completion of a challenge well met.

We had decided to spend the morning fishing in the sound and harvesting our two crab pots. We were eager to use the boat since we had adjusted the carburetor. It would hum now, with the gasoline and oil mixture just right and the idle speed slowed from its rabbit-like character.

Marvin was the name of our modest fiberglass boat. Admittedly it was a nautically unconventional name, but it is what she wanted to be called, so why not? We had had Marvin just over a year and were still in the adolescence of our nautical expertise. We had recently engaged in the initial celebration of the annual ritual of bottom scraping and painting. We had one-handedly lubed the motor (in order to hold the operations manual in the other hand). We were pleased at the sense of ownership and independence that resulted from our doing our own carburetor work.

Now we anticipated a pleasant buzz out toward No. 4 marker and a profitable morning of fishing. We looked forward to the serenity of the scene being interrupted by the tug of a fish on the line, arousing us from the enjoyable reveries of blue sky, wispy clouds and gentle breezes, with the occasional gull or pelican.

It was my turn to start Marvin and pilot us out to our destination. Mary loaded the boat with our fishing gear and snack, and skillfully disengaged us from our mooring - a salvaged rope tied to a stake in the grassy bank. With the flourish of trying a maneuver for the first time, I thrust the idling motor into reverse and we were off. For caution's sake we took a turn up the canal before heading out to the sound. After the jack-rabbit start in reverse, which almost brought the motor shaft out of the water, Marvin proceeded forward in fine style. Once when I slowed to full idle, the motor quit, but restarted easily. We finessed a gentle U-turn (nautical equivalents were still not a natural part of our vocabulary), and headed out of the canal to the sound.

Our crab pots rested close to shore. Deciding that we didn't want the crabs in the boat with us all morning, we planned to empty the pots on our return. Perhaps if we had harvested the pots first, we may have had a warning of further motor trouble, but we headed for the marker about two miles from shore.

Pamlico Sound is thirty miles wide, separating the lower part of the Outer Banks from the mainland. For a mile out, it is quite shallow, the depth varying with the winds and the tide, but is generally no deeper than three to four feet. Northwest winds may shift the sands into the canal so that a boat's prop or bottom may drag occasionally if the operator is not alert. Further out, the water gradually deepens to five, then eight and eventually twenty feet or more.

We had never taken Marvin out beyond two or three miles and we didn't go out in much wind. Our respect for weather and water was considerable, and in our nautical naiveté, we considered the weather reports and watched the waves, and chose calm, clear, stable weather for our outings.

It was such a day. A wind from the northeast at about eight miles an hour – enough to make the currents in the sound visible – invited us to find the fish there. Marvin's motor sounded smooth as we ran. We wanted it to sound smooth. After about thirty minutes, the fifteen horses of power took us to the spot we had decided to fish. Mary threw over the anchor and Marvin swung around gracefully and settled, bow to the northeast and stern to the southwest.

Straight behind us we could see familiar landmarks on shore and cars on Highway 12 headed to Hatteras Village – to the west, in the strange geography of Hatteras Island. We could identify the campground that lay in those days on both sides of the fishing pier. Two or three miles on down the road, we saw the water tower and cottages in a development facing the sound. Our own canal seemed to be about two miles to the east.

With Marvin now quiet and secured at anchor, Mary and I baited our hooks and invited the fish to bite. We split a beer and nibbled cheese. Taut anchor rope, gentle breeze, warm morning sun, a beautiful kaleidoscopic blue and white sky – we were content to lie back and watch until the pole jerked.

Such a scene is a delight – unless your chief aim is to secure fish, and the scene of serenity persists to the exclusion of any jerk on the line. So it was for us that morning: no bites, not even from the blue crabs that often tease anglers. We decided after awhile to take our business else- where. We would just cruise on back, tie up the boat and drive down to the pier to fish the remainder of the morning. We stowed our gear and prepared to weigh anchor and head home.

Ah, but Marvin seemed reluctant. The motor started eagerly, but neither forward nor reverse gear would engage. We were moving all right – but with the wind and the current, not by the grace of the motor – and we were moving toward Hatteras, not our canal!

Three more attempts to engage the gears and delight in Marvin's surge forward yielded no such results. Mary threw out the anchor again so we could assess our situation and plan our actions with more poise. Our first reaction was alarm – there were no other boats in sight. Marvin's simple style required no running lights and we had recently removed the mirror we usually kept as a signaling device. However, reason soon surfaced. If we did nothing but drift with the wind and the current, we would soon come to land – either at the campground or at an accessible shore closer to Hatteras Village.

We did have one paddle in the boat, so we could, if we chose, try for our own canal. Eventually we would even be in water shallow enough to wade and pull the boat. We didn't think much of that idea, since jellyfish were still enjoying the warm waters. Yet, it was an option.

Agreeing that we were not in any real danger, we opted for the challenge of returning to our home port via paddle power. That power was rather limited, since we had only one paddle and neither of us had ever been a canoeist. We were fortunate that the eight-mile-an-hour winds were not head-on, but at an angle to the course we needed to take to reach the canal. Its force and direction did require a great deal of muscle and maneuvering to counteract. Every time we changed paddlers, unless we dropped anchor, we would lose considerable forward progress. At that, with a twenty-five-foot anchor rope, we swung around a good bit with every change. It was not easy to keep a straight course. Inexperienced paddling tends to send a boat in a zigzag pattern at best, especially when there is only one person paddling!

Gradually, we could see progress. One after another we crossed the four-foot bands of smoother water that marked various currents in the sound. While the houses that marked the entrance to our canal appeared smaller rather than larger, we were getting closer to shore and into more shallow water. How glad we were that this was a morning fishing trip and not one graced by the beauties of a sunset – followed by darkness!

All signs of fear had disappeared; signs of fatigue were in ascendancy. The periods of paddling before anchoring and shifting power were becoming briefer, conversation grew sparse, and rest periods a bit stretched. Optimistically, we still measured progress. We might get to shore a mile below the entrance to the canal, but the shore was closer – one couldn't use the word "looming" – but it was discernibly more nearly in reach. We could make it.

Closer to shore, we expected to have, with the protection of land, less wind to confront and easier progress. However, our slight knowledge of the sound's contours did not include familiarity with the slough that hugs the shore, with a pretty strong current in it – and this was the last barrier to the mouth of our canal.

New tactics were called for! We pressed into service our landing net; while the person in the stern paddled, the other in the bow poled. It took quite a few tries, with not a little bit of frustration reflected in language and posture, to find the necessary coordination of those two techniques of propulsion. We even dredged up scraps of old chanteys to encourage coordination – no such simple ones as the bo'sun's *stroke!* for a shell crew, nor the *yo heave ho!* of the Volga boatmen, but more like a gasping plea for joint effort. Also, poling worked only in water of a particular depth, given the length of the landing net's handle.

Had anyone been watching the scene with binoculars, surely they would have had trouble steadying their hand for laughing at our antics. We must have been a wonder to behold. At last it seemed to be only a hundred yards to go to the canal entrance. Only! That is the length of a football field, and the current in the slough was losing none of its strength. We didn't have the nerve to go out further from shore to escape it – that seemed too defeating, so we continued our zigzagging pattern slowly forward.

At last we were within two boat-lengths of the canal, then were able to escape the current and squeeze into the canal's welcome quiet water. Our speed now seemed breathtaking! In spite of our nearly exhausted reservoir of endurance, we spurted ahead with new vigor – not to mention exhilaration.

Usually our maneuvering to our "dock" took some care in executing a ninety-degree turn in toward the bank, cutting the motor at just the right time to avoid throwing the anchor person ashore or else leaving too great a gap for mooring to be possible. I had had two experiences of sending the boat out from under me by trying to step over too big a gap! Today, there was no such problem. The turn was easily handled and we crept close to the bank. Never had that mooring spot looked so secure as it did on that day.

We had done it! We had brought ourselves in! We had used muscles we hardly knew we had, and they were adequate. Though we had been out probably only two miles, the wind and current and our measure of strength combined to create a course that must have stretched our paddling distance to at least three miles. It took us some three hours to return home, but to our amazement and joy, neither of us suffered any sore muscles nor sunburn from our ordeal.

There should have been a photographer to capture our triumphant return to port, but we have been satisfied with the mental images of our great voyage. ❦

Hatteras Haiku

Bettie Currie

Pelicans skim waves
Wings almost touch the water
But never get wet.

The tide is rising
It gently washes the shells
Then backs out to sea.

A tern hovers first
Then dives swiftly, wings folded
Then rises again.

Thick tracks in the sand
From two agile 4x4s
Make tan tweed patterns.

The sun shines on us
Two old women at the beach.
Gives form to haiku.

Stephanie Kiker Geib

Stephanie Kiker Geib is a graphic designer and illustrator who grew up in Statesville, North Carolina and earned her degree in graphic design from North Carolina State University. In 1985, as a sophomore, she interned at the North Carolina Aquarium in Manteo, designing displays. Stephanie and her husband, Scott, who is a photographer, own Light Keeper Gallery in Hatteras Village. The gallery features the exclusive art and photography of this husband-and-wife team. Stephanie's emphasis is on the local wildlife and scenery, which drew her to Hatteras Island along with the "laid back" lifestyle. The area also has kept Stephanie busy with her graphic design work.

Priscilla Hine DeLong

Priscilla Hine DeLong lived in Frisco with her husband and two daughters. She was an artist, famous for her riotous "Menopausal Mermaid" sculptures, and a photographer who volunteered her talent at Cape Hatteras School. An avid windsurfer, she wrote several columns for "The Island Breeze" newspaper, exploring her passion for the sport. Priscilla died on July 20, 2001 at her residence, and is remembered well for her loyal friendship, her contagious laughter and her intent to make every day of her life a joyous celebration.

We Don't Need to be Wind Whiners

Priscilla Hine DeLong

The only thing better than waking up to a brilliant and sunny twenty-mile-per-hour-plus wind day on Hatteras Island is waking up to a glorious day without even the slightest whisper of wind. The eerie, even calm of the Pamlico Sound is so surreal and complete that you are unable to see where the sky stops and the water begins. The world is enormous in this stillness.

Your sails are all rigged, neatly stacked and ready to go. Just one thing missing. We don't need to whine about the lack of wind because days like this are special gifts. Even for us wind addicts. Receive it graciously and use it wisely. This is quite a rare occurrence. Enjoy it.

Birds can be heard trilling proudly in this deafening quiet. You can feel the dragonfly wing vibrations as these palm-sized creatures dive-bomb you in their uninterrupted dances. Each little movement underwater is clearly evident on the surface. Each ripple evokes imaginative ideas of just what might be happening under there.

Pamlico Sound is a wonder-filled arena for all sorts of adventures. On these quiet days, I hear the muffled screams of every kayak on the island yelling to be put into the water and taken for a ride. What an opportunity!

If you are quiet, you will be amazed at the secrets that can be revealed. Kayaks are available all over Hatteras, but if you find yourself with no access to a kayak, consider some serious (up to your waist) wading.

You will be surprised at how shallow these waters really are, and that in most areas you can wade out at least five hundred yards to waist-deep water. (Yes, I am short.) This is a real chance to see just what the bottom looks like that you normally scream over on a windy day.

Grab this chance to investigate the awesome creatures of these shallows and the underwater landscape that is their home. "Sound Stomps" have been a mainstay activity in our household since we moved here. While many mysteries have been explained, others have presented themselves and remain unsolved and unpredictable.

Good swim shoes or old sneakers are a must as the bottom is littered with oyster shells, many of them with oysters happily living in them. Oyster shell cuts require extra cleaning care and may take a long time to heal. This can put a real cramp in your sailing style. An ounce of prevention is worth its weight in gold.

Crabs skitter sideways out of your path with Mach-fear speed, and flounder will blow their almost perfect camouflage in a puff of sand smoke. Skates of all sizes may soar past you, making your heart skip a beat. These creatures are harmless and are the source of those bizarre swirls and white flashes in the corner of your vision while you are windsurfing.

Bird watching takes on new meaning after you see, first hand, the drama and carnage of osprey, egrets or herons hunting and fishing. Pamlico Sound becomes the theater. It is wonderful entertainment and another reward for a windless day.

The egrets and herons show us patience in their paralyzed fishing stance, as well as power in their lightning-bolt, spearing speed. They are not shy and will fish right in front of you as long as you remain relatively calm and quiet. Their bills are quite impressive when viewed close.

Osprey are more elusive and can be seen circling and searching the sound waters with their keen vision. They literally, just before impact with the water, fold in half to grab their prey, claw first. It is awesome. Sometimes they catch fish in their clutch backwards and, while shaking the water off their feathers, they also must turn the fish around in their clasp so that it is aerodynamically correct. Seeing this makes you believe it!

Other unbelievable things occur in these calms as well. Without the concurrence of family and friends, I would have doubted whether one adventure, in fact, really happened to us. It was a moonless, motionless summer night without a breath of wind to mark the water surface. Quite by accident, I was looking into the dark Sound from a dock, when I noticed a gentle, greenish glow around each dock piling. Looking more closely, I realized it was phosphorescence, activated by the barnacles sweeping the water around each piling. I was stunned!

I am not sure I can adequately describe the hilarity that followed. Eight adults and ten children, fed, washed, clean, dry and ready for bed, became eighteen wet, hollering swimmers experiencing "glow in the dark" Hatteras style. Open fingers pulled through the water produced Grateful Dead light trails. Crabs running away from us in terror only managed to light their paths brilliantly. Fish darting even at distances lit up the water with large bright green slashes of light. Wearing goggles gave an even eerier perspective of all of us crashing about in the nighttime sound. Each and every hair on our arm was lit and glowed in minute detail. It was bizarre! It was unreal. It was magic!

I often think back to that evening and hope to see it again. I believe there are lots of other secrets that will be revealed in time. I need only be here. Enjoy all the gifts this fine island has to offer. Make the most of your time here.

Wind or no wind, Hatteras has its own heartbeat. Listen and adjust to it; only then may its secrets, mysteries and magic be revealed fully to you. ⚓

This was first published in *The Island Breeze*, June 1998

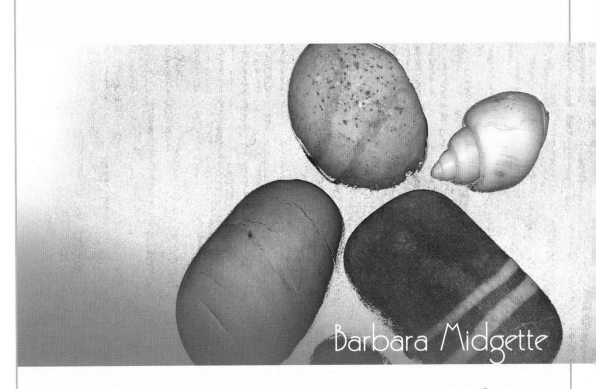

Barbara Midgette

Barbara Midgette is the widow of L. G. Midgette of Buxton, North Carolina
She was born in Washington, D.C., where she attended the American University.
She lived in Mexico City for a time, worked in the music division of the D.C.
Public Library and was program specialist in the music division of the Pan American
Union. Moving to Hatteras Island in 1970, she worked at Cape Hatteras
School in several areas, including the school library, and taught Spanish to a gifted
and talented class. She wrote a children's play in Spanish that class members
performed at the school. She joined the staff of Buxton Village Books when it
opened in 1984. She has three grown sons and still lives in Buxton.

*This story is a condensation of part I of a novella in progress. The novella follows the further
adventures of Cane, Sumner and Robin as well as Cane's sister, Laney, and a stranger who
isn't what he seems. Other friends and family populate the story, as does a teacher who turns out
to be important to them all.*

*Although some of the characters in this story are based on real people with real names, the
actions attributed to them are the product of the author's imagination and are purely fictitious,
as is the story itself. Real place names are used fictitiously.*

Cane's Hatteras Alligator

Barbara Midgette

When Cane went fishing in a lighthouse pond that summer day, he had hope. School wouldn't start for a long time, and his best friend was beside him, their California surfer-style, dyed blond buzz cuts shining in the sunlight. They were twelve years old and full of pride.

"Sumner?" Cane called to his buddy, "I think I like this Flower's Ridge pond best." Sumner nodded in agreement. He accepted Cane, who always had the best ideas, as the natural leader of their joint expeditions.

"I brought some of my dad's treble hooks. Snagging can bring up some weird stuff sometimes."

"Well, all I've got is this little trout rod. It won't handle trash like old inner tubes." Sumner was as wary as usual.

"Nothing like that in here. Maybe a big turtle. Hey, wouldn't a snapping turtle be cool?" Cane was his normal, cocky self.

Both boys focused on their tackle. Just one of the treble hook's three barbs would grab almost any hapless creature encountered on the pond's slimy bottom.

This pond was one of several in the area, all distinguished by fresh water instead of salt like the ocean or brackish like Pamlico Sound. A truly enormous storm could crowd tons of saltwater up over the beach, causing it to run all over everything in sight, including the fresh-water ponds, but this kind of storm was rare even here at weather-beaten Cape Hatteras. The pond was surrounded by a smooth, green grass meadow overhung with the drooping branches of leafy swamp willow trees, their shade welcome on this steaming July day. The boys felt grateful for the shelter as they made their first casts into the middle of the murky water.

Many lazy lobs later, Sumner threw his rod and himself down on the grass in disgust.

"Too hot! Got a drink?"

"Yeah, sure. In my backpack. Where's yours?"

"Forgot."

"Not again!"

As Sumner ambled over toward Cane's pack, out the corner of his eye he saw Cane abruptly shift his weight and dig his heels sharply into the ground. Like Sumner, Cane had wearied of standing in the heat and had sat down at the edge of the pond. He was day dreaming of alligator snapping turtles when he felt a heavy, dead weight on his line. He automatically set the hook and began the laborious process of hauling in what was sure to be a piece of trash, maybe the inner tube he had promised Sumner wasn't there. Within a few minutes, he began to sweat, his T-shirt turning into a hot, slimy trap.

"What in the world do you have?"

"Don't know. Doesn't feel alive."

"Hah!" crowed Sumner gleefully.

After some twenty minutes and a terrible struggle, Cane felt himself weaken. His arms and hands stopped doing his bidding.

"Sumner! Come here! I'm too tired and this might be alive. I keep feeling twitches and I don't want to cut the line and give up yet. If you'll take over for me, I'll get a drink and rest for while."

Reacting to Cane's obvious exhaustion, Sumner moved quickly. As he took over, he could feel the pull of a great weight.

"You're right. There is something on here. I'll keep reeling while you rest. Then maybe between us we can get it in to shore. Sumner fought the invisible weight as hard as he could for another twenty minutes. Cane got to his feet when he saw Sumner start to fade. He got a shock when he felt the great power of the pulling. He decided right then that he was no match for whatever this was. Discouraged, he held on as the drag on his reel began to slip. He knew that if he tightened it the line would snap.

"This is a monster! I'll hold it as long as I can and maybe we can get a glimpse of it. I'd hate to lose it without at least seeing it."

What neither Cane nor Sumner knew was that their prey actually weighed more than sixty pounds and was over seven feet long. The twitching they were feeling came from spasms of pain. Two of the three sharp hooks were so deeply imbedded that the barbs held their grip even as the animal tried to escape the terrible stinging in its foot. It was worn out and desperate.

The heat was starting to make Cane feel sick. He was soaking wet. All his Gatorade had turned into sweat and he knew he couldn't take much more. The air was steaming and the sun felt like fire on his skin.

"I've got an idea. If you'll hang on to the rod, I'll try to get close enough to grab the line, and then pull on it with my hands. Maybe that will change its direction and get it in closer. It's so slow it's as if it doesn't have much more strength than we do." As Sumner held on, Cane moved to the pond's edge and grabbed the line, angling it to his right.

Later, when he tried to tell people about what had happened, he remembered the next moment best – the slow, sluggish shift in direction as the beast began to come toward him. He was too excited to breathe. Tired of the struggle, the pain in its foot unbearable, a shiny, black, armor-plated alligator dragged itself up on shore, favoring its hooked and injured webbed foot as it moved.

"SUMNER! Run NOW and get help from one of the rangers at the lighthouse! If Miss Marcia's there, get her! RUN! RUN!" Sumner took off running as fast as his tired, hot legs would allow, so charged up he couldn't feel his feet. The driver of a passing car saw his distress and stopped to give him a ride. At the museum building, he jumped from the car with an over the shoulder thanks and ran calling for Miss Marcia or anyone else who would come to help. She was there and on her way almost before Sumner had a chance to explain. He had to run to keep up with her.

"I think we're going to need more than just you because this alligator is longer than you are tall!"

She pulled out her cell phone and Sumner heard her mutter something about "just in case."

"O.K. Mary's coming too as soon as she can. Her seven-year-old daughter, Foster, is with her today so they'll both be there."

The alligator was clearly visible as Miss Marcia slowed down and stopped some distance away. She called Mary again and told her to be quiet and careful. Cane was so glad to see them he had to stop himself from yelling.

A pathetic sight met their eyes. Sumner thought of a starving puppy he had once seen, and Marcia thought of the vet. This was Thursday, which meant that Dr. Matthew was on Hatteras Island in his office van, attending to sick pets. Miss Marcia's inquiries found him in Frisco; he would arrive in ten minutes.

The reptile had collapsed into the mud and Cane finally felt safe enough to let go of the fishing line. The tormented beast took no notice. It looked barely conscious.

Suddenly out of nowhere, Foster came into view, streaking straight for the alligator's hurt foot. Before anyone could stop her, she was on her knees much too close for safety. But Dr. Matthew had also arrived and he moved swiftly to the water's edge, crouching down beside Foster and pulling her back. He then opened his bag which contained, among other valuable tools, wire cutters and pliers. While Miss Marcia held the animal's mouth closed, he cut the hooks and threaded them out backwards so they wouldn't catch and tear the flesh. Foster was so relieved, she told Dr. Matthew she wanted to be a vet when she grew up.

Soon a small audience gathered and major discussions began about what to do.

Noticing how sad Cane looked, Dr. Matthew walked over to give him a pat on the shoulder before heading for Hatteras to vaccinate a couple of mustangs. Cane was definitely sad. He didn't want to lose his alligator and that was about to happen. The rangers had figured out that the safest place was Milltail Creek past Buffalo City within the Alligator River National Refuge near the red wolf pens in mainland Dare County.

"If you're going to take him someplace, I want to go with him to make sure he's all right. After all, he's my alligator!" Cane told Miss Marcia miserably.

"Let's call your mom and see what she thinks."

Cane's mom, Robin, responded quickly. "Why, of course!"

The next step was to involve U.S. Fish and Wildlife since the alligator would be under their protection. They would be the ones seeing to the actual transport. Cane and his mother would follow right behind. Miss Marcia wanted to let Dr. Matthew know what they were planning and caught up with him in Hatteras Village as he was finishing his work there. She was not surprised to hear that he had every intention of joining the small caravan as it made its way to Milltail Creek.

After they had arrived at a good, wet spot, the unloading took place. Cane saw that his alligator was now quite alert. In fact, Cane became so unnerved by the sight of all eighty of its enormous, cone-shaped teeth that he stepped back abruptly.

"Is he gonna bite?" he asked Dr Matthew.

"I think not. He's still tired and confused and probably needs a nap before eating anything. I brought a raw chicken with me. We can leave it where it can be seen and smelled in case he wakes up hungry. Let's leave him in peace for now."

With Dr. Matthew at his side to answer his questions, Cane tried his best to learn everything he could about alligators.

"Well, the first thing is size. At seven feet long, this one is at least eight years old, and it will keep on growing for a long time if nothing happens to it. Some grow to be nineteen feet long, and the males are larger than the females."

"So what does he do when the weather gets cold? Go somewhere warmer?"

"Nope. He'll dig himself a hole about as deep as you are tall, get in it and stay there until his body tells him it's warm enough to come out. He might get pneumonia if he suddenly gets too cold."

"Can he breathe under water?"

"No, but he can close his nostrils tightly when he needs to be under water."

"Can he hear? Does he have ears?"

"Yes indeed. You can't see them, but they're right behind his eyes, hidden behind a leathery plate that he can open or close whenever he wants. There are hinge valves near his eyes. He needs to keep his ears protected when he's under water so as not to hurt or rupture his ear drums."

"What about his eyes? He can see under water, right?"

"He's got another neat trick to protect his eyes under water. It's called a nictitating membrane, and since it's transparent, the alligator can see just fine. He has to be able to see under water otherwise he wouldn't be able to hunt for food."

It was time to go home. They had done all there was to be done. Saying their final goodbyes, they departed one vehicle at a time, bouncing along the deeply rutted and potholed road. Dr. Matthew said a special goodbye to Cane and told him he hoped they'd see each other soon.

Cane was quiet for most of the trip home to Buxton. After awhile he wanted to know when they could go back to make sure his alligator was O.K.

"I've been thinking about that myself," his mother answered. "I think probably right after the worst of the hurricane season – maybe in early October."

"That sounds about right to me, too. Maybe he'll still be where we left him, but that refuge is huge and there's an awful lot of water. He could move anytime, at least until the weather gets too cold."

"We're certainly not going to forget your alligator after a day like today, are we?" Cane didn't answer. He was sound asleep and he didn't wake when Robin pulled into their driveway. She had never seen him this tired. She had a hard time believing a couple of twelve-year-old kids did what he and Sumner had done. She even looked forward to October herself. It would be so exciting if the alligator were still where they could come to see it. She found herself thinking of the creature as a "he" and not an "it" at all, and understood for the first time why people kept baby alligators in their bathtubs as pets. Had Cane's alligator been a pet that had grown too big for someone's bathtub? It seemed quite possible. She must remember to pick up a couple of raw chickens when the time came for their next visit!

Cane was so tired that he slept late for several days after the trip. On the third morning, he found Sumner sitting beside his bed waiting for him to wake up. He could hear the soothing sounds of booming surf.

"What happened to you, man? You flat out disappeared after the rangers got to the pond."

"My dad came by and needed me to go with him to help with some nets and by the time we were finished, everyone had left, including the alligator."

Cane told Sumner about the alligator's new home, and everything he had learned from Dr. Matthew. He also mentioned the planned October trip. "This time you'll come with us. We'll go on a Saturday when there's no school." This was not a question, but a statement, and it got no argument from Sumner.

That settled, they grabbed some Nabs peanut butter crackers and a couple of bottles of Gatorade and set out for the beach to look for treasure. An offshore storm had created heavy seas and given the shore a pounding, a good predictor of odd stuff washing up to be left stranded when the tide went out. Of all the strange things they had found, the favorite in Cane's beach collection was an empty black and white squirt canister with a drawing on its label of a large louse lying on its back, its legs in the air. Since all the writing was in Russian, Cane could only guess that a nearby Russian ship, maybe a submarine, had been infested with lice. There was only one word on it that used what appeared to be English alphabet letters, but probably weren't. 'TAPAKAHOB' it said. Another storm had produced sea beans carried north from tropical waters. They were by far the biggest beans Cane had ever seen – a couple of inches wide and half an inch thick with hard, glossy hulls the color of mahogany. Cane had kept these for his beach collection too except for the one his dad had planted. Nothing came up. Would it have looked like Jack's beanstalk in the fairy tale? Cane wondered.

School started after Labor Day and was usually in full swing before the first big hurricane of the season. Cane hated it when high water in Pamlico Sound spilled over its banks and filled up the driveway. Then his mom would have to find high ground for the car. During Hurricane Emily, cars had floated in the parking lot at the bank. This year turned out to be a lucky one and although there was plenty of wind, rain and tide, nothing scary happened and the big storms either kept their distance offshore or made glancing passes and headed northeast out to sea. No one had to evacuate.

Cane began counting the days until the first Saturday in October.

"Did you stop by Conner's to make sure they have plenty of chickens?" he asked his mom. "I think we should take three big whole ones. Will that be enough?" His mother laughed. She was looking forward to next Saturday too.

"What about our lunch? Can we take a picnic? We've got to have potato salad! That's the most important thing and after that, deviled eggs. Sumner and I like ham and mustard sandwiches. Apples are already here from the mountains, and baby cut carrots will take care of the vegetable part."

"Sounds to me as if you've already decided on the menu. How would you like it if I baked a chocolate fudge cake – the kind with the icing made of nothing but semi-sweet chocolate with butter and vanilla?" The answer was in his face.

Cane needed to get in touch with Sumner. He hadn't been in school for a couple of days and even though the trip had been planned and discussed endlessly, his absences made Cane feel uneasy. If he didn't answer his phone this evening, Cane would have to go to his house tomorrow afternoon.

The next morning found Sumner back at school. He seemed fine. He had been helping his father with drop-net gear, getting ready for the fall run. Since this kind of fishing was done from a small boat fairly near the ocean beach, everything had to be just right or an accident could easily happen. All it took was one tall, steep, shore-breaking wave and over you went, along with the gear and the whole stash of other items in the boat, not to mention the boat itself. Sumner was proud of how much help he was to his father. In fact, without noticing, he was learning to be a skilled drop netter himself. Cane reminded him again that Saturday was just a couple of days away and they would need to pick him up at 10 o'clock. It was hard to think about schoolwork, but they both did their best and no one seemed to notice their missing brains during the map study project.

Saturday morning finally arrived, and Cane was awake at first light. He stayed quiet until he could hear his mother stirring and then jumped out of bed. There were still a few things to take care of before they left to pick up Sumner.

"Ready?" Cane's mom asked.

"I think so, but I forgot drinks. Did you remember them?"

"Yup! We're out of here."

They pulled into Sumner's driveway five minutes later, only to find it empty and the house closed. Cane's spirits fell. So many times recently, Sumner had either disappeared or never shown up at all. He ran up the steps and banged on the door, but there was no sign of anyone at home. Cane gave up and got back in the car, defeated.

"Mom, why does Sumner keep doing this? I don't get it."

"I'm quite sure it has nothing to do with you and everything to do with his father. I think you'll discover later that there was a serious net emergency – something so bad it put the whole fishing season at risk. And he can't call you if he's not home or it's four o'clock in the morning. He just couldn't come, that's all. Now, come on and let's hope there's an alligator waiting for us!"

They stopped for fuel at Cane's dad's gas station and after a few minutes were again on their way. Cane's dad, Ken, had gone off with his partner, Jarvis, to pull out a truck caught as the tide crept up unnoticed at Cape Point. They had taken the new heavy tow truck, knowing they'd find yet another stuck vehicle and its frantic owner. Ken and Jarvis had many photographs of trucks they had rescued mounted on the paneling of their sales counter, some sunk up to their axles in beach sand, others with surf breaking against the doors. There had been a few embarrassing times when even the new and powerful tow truck had sunk its rear axle in red sand, the most treacherous sand of all.

Before long they were on the long stretch of Highway 12 past the S curve with the bridge over Oregon Inlet coming up fast. Cane looked with longing at the charter boats as they drove past the fishing center. Most slips were empty, the charter boats offshore after blue and white marlin, sailfish, yellow fin tuna and mahi mahi. Although Cane's dad still called it dolphin, Robin thought the name had been changed so that people wouldn't confuse it with porpoise when it was served on a restaurant dinner plate.

They turned left onto Highway 64 at Whalebone Junction. Cane began to wiggle and bounce in his seat, driving his mother crazy. Milltail Creek was only a half hour away.

"Look, Mom, there's the Buffalo City sign. We need to turn here and would you believe what a mess this road is, full of potholes and mud?"

Robin shifted gears down into low, hoping her faithful old car wouldn't get stuck, and in they went.

"Tell me when you think we're close to where we put him in. There was a pond, and water in a wetland with an open field next to it. There's a parking area at the landing where we can stop and eat lunch. Afterwards we can walk back to the place you think he's most likely to be." Cane had forgotten about the picnic lunch packed in the cooler, but now began to feel really hungry. He started to relax. This was so much fun! They sat down on a log to enjoy their lunch.

"I'm trying to think where I would like to be if I were an alligator and I'm pretty sure it would be in that pond we passed. It has nice, gooey edges but looks deep enough in the middle and it's got marsh grass all around it," said Cane. "What do you think?"

Robin had no idea how it would feel to be an alligator and so decided to leave where to look up to Cane.

"Let's get this lunch cleaned up and start walking," she said. "Grab those chickens. We may find a hungry reptile!"

"I don't think we should talk. If either of us sees anything moving, we can tap each other's hand. Let's go as quietly as we can, very slowly."

They were walking toward Cane's idea of the alligator's home, when Robin found herself stopping in the middle of the road.

"Wait! This is a big and dangerous animal! I'm sure he can move very quickly when he feels threatened. Let's stop and listen every few minutes. I know we'll hear him. I doubt there's anything quiet about an agitated alligator on the move."

Side by side, they walked slowly, stopping and hearing nothing but ordinary insect buzzes and a few bird calls. When they arrived in the area near the pond, Cane unwrapped the chickens and set them down, then backed off to where they could hide themselves behind a large, leafy red bay without being seen by their quarry. Rigid with tension and expecting a long vigil, they settled down to wait. *Scritch, scritch.* Robin was the first to hear the tiny whispery sound that was barely there. Then Cane heard it, made a shushing gesture, and began to creep toward the sound, beckoning his mother to follow him. Before long, they came upon a long path of flattened grass. Cane saw waving marsh grasses beside the pond where he had put down the chickens. Cane was completely fearless, but Robin knew their prey was a wild and unpredictable reptile with a brain the size of a sea bean and full of instincts unrelated to Cane's affection, mainly finding food. For all she knew, Cane might look like a much better meal than raw chicken! As she was considering this unpleasant possibility, a large narrow head appeared at the end of the path. Cane thought he would pass out from joy, but Robin thought she might do the same from sheer terror. The alligator was now turning all the way around to face his visitors.

"Wait. Don't forget we're downwind of him," Cane murmured as the beast regarded them with what looked like polite interest. It began to move slowly toward them, bobbing its head gently up and down as if extending a friendly and personal greeting. Cane was beside himself. They held their ground as the creature continued its slow and labored walk down the path. When it felt it had come close enough, it stopped, gave a final nod, turned slowly around and crept back to where it had come from. At the end of the path near the pond, it looked back once. Cane was sure it smiled.

Robin let out her breath in a huge gasp. "Fantastic!" was all she could say. Cane was unable to speak, his eyes wide and round, his mouth forming a surprised O!

"Time to go."

Cane was so dazed that Robin had to guide him to the car. He felt as if he were in a dream on the ride home, the fading light revealing an eerie world of variously shaped wind-splayed cedars, skeletons of pine trees consumed by pine bark beetles, bristly water bushes and fields of purple grasses as they drove down the highway toward Buxton.

🦐 🦐 🦐

The winter was cold. It rained a lot and even snowed twice. Several times the wind blew from the northeast, strong enough and long enough for sea tide to sink the highway south of the S curve. Tall trucks passed through the salt water with care, going under five miles an hour, creating no wake and keeping the water off their undersides. Local people always undercoated their trucks and cars to protect them from salt and were truly astonished each time some hotdogger passed them going full blast, throwing salt everywhere and guaranteeing serious damage to their new forty-thousand-dollar pride and joy, not to mention similar harm to the vehicles they overtook in such a burst of salt and glory.

"I'll bet that alligator of mine has dug down deep to keep warm by now," Cane commented to his mother one morning.

"I certainly would!" was her reply. She too was cold a lot of the time these days and already looking forward to the warmer days ahead.

After a cold and snowy Christmas holiday, school started again with sickening intensity. The work was so hard that neither Cane nor Sumner had time to think about anything else. By Easter break, the workload eased and Cane started bugging his mom about getting back to Milltail. She would have none of it. The weather was still terrible.

"Not only will the highway be sunk, but that bad road full of potholes will be full of water too. Besides, the alligator is still warm and cozy in his hole. Why would he want to come out now, for Pete's sake?"

"But Mom. . ."

"No! I mean NO! Talk to me again around the end of May, and we need to clear any trip with Sumner's dad in advance. Don't forget what kept happening last fall."

Robin didn't forget about Sumner's father. In mid May, she went to see him, determined to find a time that would work for all of them and not get cancelled and disappoint the boys again. He thought it over for a few minutes before telling her he couldn't promise anything until early August. Now everyone would know what to expect. Although August was a long way off, at least it was definite. Sumner would finally be able to join them.

In what seemed like no time school was out for the summer. Seventh grade had turned out to be rough, but both boys had done well and felt confident about managing the coming school year. Summer meant freedom that felt like forever and the promise of a trip to Milltail. June and July were hot and full of adventures and fun, but it was August that beckoned.

They settled on a Wednesday and Robin decided to do a repeat of last year's picnic, including a raw chicken lunch for the alligator.

Sumner was waiting impatiently on his porch when Robin and Cane went to pick him up.

"Thought you'd never get here!" he exclaimed. "Mosquitoes are thick. Did you bring a can of repellent?"

"Can't have that stuff stinking up our clothes. No alligator would want us near him. We want to get up CLOSE!"

This thought silenced Sumner for a few minutes. "How close are you planning on getting?" he finally dared to ask.

"Close as we can without spooking him. If he runs away and hides, we'll never find him." Sumner seemed satisfied with this explanation, but remained suspicious.

Robin and the boys took off, pleased to be all together again after such a long wait. Cane spent the drive time to Milltail explaining how they did everything, the slow walking, the hand tap signal, the red bay and anything else he could think of.

The picnic was much better with Sumner there. They stuffed themselves with so much cake that they needed a walk to burn if off. Sumner was elected to carry the raw chicken. Cane thought if the alligator could smell Sumner on it, he would know who he was. Robin thought that Sumner looked like as good an alligator dinner as Cane had the last time they were here. After putting the chickens down where Cane showed him, Sumner scooted back to the red bay as fast as he could quietly go. They waited a good half hour before Cane heard what he was sure was a faint sound. "Hear that? Hear that?" he whispered to the others. Robin and Sumner strained to hear and after a few minutes Sumner heard a tiny scratching noise. He thought he heard little peeping sounds too. All this waiting was making him so nervous he was quivering.

"Mom, I can't see a thing!" complained Cane. "I've got to get at least a little closer." Robin didn't like this idea one bit, but did agree with Cane that they seemed too far away. She agreed to move forward another twenty-five feet or so. She kept hearing a soft sound that sounded like birds peeping.

They had moved no more than twenty feet up the path when they discovered to their horror that even this short distance had put them much too close. They looked with terror at the alligator on top of what appeared to be a huge nest, slamming its head from side to side, snapping its jaws full of those terrible yellow teeth and thrashing its heavy tail with an awful power.

Sumner fainted.

"You idiot!" cried Cane, opening his drink and pouring it in his friend's face. He was furious that Sumner was missing the sight of an enraged alligator on top of its nest and not only that, there were a least fifty tiny alligator babies milling around what had to be their mother and peeping intently. They couldn't have been more than eight inches long. Cane's alligator was a girl?

Sumner was coming to, and Cane and his mom wanted to get him up and far enough back to allow the mother alligator to calm down. They began retreating, their eyes never leaving the nest, hoping she would stop all this thrashing and gnashing business. After a few minutes the commotion ended, but the peeping got louder. They had come upon her at the very moment that the babies were hatching from their buried eggs. She had been busy tearing up the nest to let them out so she could lead them into the pond.

"Sumner, you take it easy now, honey, or you're going to miss something you may never get to see again as long as you live," Robin cautioned.

Robin and Cane stood on either side of Sumner as the three of them gazed at the splendid sight. Robin was tall enough to see the alligator turn and, with the babies following closely, move down the side of the three-and-a-half-foot-tall nest mound toward the water. Cane was able to convince Sumner they needed to climb the red bay in the hope it would hold their weight. What they then saw was incredible. All the babies were being led down the side of the mound and into the water by their mother. She waited until every single one of them had made it to safety and then disappeared. Her job as a mother was finished just like that!

Robin and her charges would have clapped and cheered had they not feared annoying the mother alligator again. They knew they had just witnessed a rare and magical event, one they understood would never come to any one of them again.

The mother alligator had settled down out of sight for a well-deserved nap, but Cane didn't care. He was so ecstatic he needed nothing more from this day.

They walked on air the entire way back to the car. Sumner was the most affected.

He felt as if he had suddenly been transported into the middle of an African safari. Fainting had made him weird anyway and the combination of events was putting him somewhere up in high, cottony clouds. He had nothing to say, but followed Cane and Robin automatically.

The silence in the car during the ride home was absolute. Not one of the three said a word.

"See ya," was all Sumner could get out when they dropped him off at his house. It was close to supper-time and lights were on in the kitchen and dining room. He could see his mother through the window as he came up the steps. It was almost dark and although they had been gone only a few hours, to Sumner it could have been days and he wouldn't have known the difference.

Robin was filled with a delight that would last for a long time. How reasonably everything had worked out. She knew a perfect ending when she saw one, and was glad to her very bones.

Cane, however, saw the matter a little differently. Always practical and thinking ahead, he was gratified to see before him an endless supply of alligators – enough to last him a lifetime. He also understood that as time went on and he got older, he could manage to get to Milltail whenever he had the need and that his very own alligator would still be his friend in the years to come, even if she was a girl! 🐊

Lynne Hoffman Foster

Lynne Hoffman Foster spent much of her previous life abroad, first
as a flight attendant and later as a marketing executive, traveling
extensively throughout the world and living in England, the Middle
East and Africa. Since moving back to the States, she has studied
at the College of the Albemarle and the University of North
Carolina at Chapel Hill. She continues her studies there via their
Independent Studies program from her home in Hatteras Village,
where she also stays busy as development director for the
Graveyard of the Atlantic Museum. She and her husband, Ernie, a
native Hatteras charter boat captain, own and operate the historic
Albatross Fleet.

The Dowager

Lynne Hoffman Foster

Tucked away within the sober village, a brief bicycle ride down the remains of a short lane, is a packed earthen bridge. It crosses a shallow creek onto a hummock. The small hummock is not far from the sound's shoreline as it rises slightly above a marsh. There on the hummock in the marsh is an old house. The house has her back turned toward the Pamlico waters and the prevailing winds. Meandering around three of her sides, barely visible beneath unmown grass grown tall, runs the little creek.

Wild yucca bloom white and high where sour apples once grew. Not even an outline remains of an Irish potato field or a goose pound. The tough old fig tree has retired and in the shallows near shore the clam stakes have rotted and crumbled and the dust has floated away; the pile of shells is turning into coarse sand. Only two broken juniper clothesline posts still stand in what was once the yard – but the old cotton line rotted away long ago. There are no scrubbed shirts or sheets to dry and freshen in the breeze, no nets to reweave. There is no domesticity, no industry in the air.

The once-pretty house is aging without grace, but interestingly, in the manner of an eccentric aging Southern woman. In the light of day she appears merely unkempt and unconcerned with appearances. When sundown gilds the remaining window glass, she is positively intriguing, flirtatiously beckoning one closer. By last light, when little but her form can be seen, a brooding darkness is revealed, as chilling as a night alone on a moor.

Where once the house hosted laughter and argument, now there is only silence broken by swooshes and screeches and the rattle of loose wooden boards when the wind passes through. A banshee seems to have moved in alongside the resident night owl, and menacing water moccasins prevent the entry of even the bold feral cats prowling the sorry places in the village.

Something strange happens when a house is no longer inhabited. It is as if the house loses its will as it loses its purpose. It ceases to hold itself upright and takes on a hunchbacked persona. Its strength diminishes daily as it sheds its useless elements. The house on the hummock sags and fades to the uneven gray of old age. What is left of rickety shutters barely protect crumbling window frames and broken panes. There no longer is a need to shade slipcovers from the relentless summer sun or to stand guard against terrible Atlantic storms. Front porch posts lean inward, threatening to spill the roof into the front room. Where wind has whipped away cedar shingles, the skeleton of the house has turned to paper. Rotting floor boards give way and finally sink, challenging access to a door locked when the final resident, a lone woman, was carried out by village men to her family cemetery. Now her burial ground too is sliding beneath the weight of time and tide.

Never again will the door open to catch a cooling breeze or admit a caring neighbor. Nor will the aroma of crabs stewing or shad baking settle over the kitchen table precisely at noon. There is no one left to walk to the docks for the daily gift of dinner from the fishermen. Nothing but a rusting old stove is left standing in the back kitchen anyway. The frequent whir of the Singer ceased long ago and the old upright piano will never again accompany a solitary soprano. It is said the old hymns could be heard throughout the village on a still evening when the spirit moved the old woman to melodious prayer.

Flowery curtains that once billowed in the salted breeze have been reduced to rags and the furnishings are now long gone, carted away like salvage from a shipwreck. The red roses that clambered over the roof in spring were lost when Hurricane Emily carried tidewater to places where flood had never been seen before.

The island and the sea are free to reclaim the hummock and the marsh. The spindly blades of grass belong to the redwings that perch precariously atop them, and large, lumbering snapping turtles own the creek and its creatures. A fat raccoon strolls comfortably across the porch, as secure as the red hawk and the otter family who also hunt there. A few oysters are taking hold again in the undisturbed shallows, but they are nearly as rare as scallops now.

Soon there will be no trace of the lane and the creek will be well hidden. One day, inevitably, the wonderful, tough, old house will finally go down with dignity, like the many ships along this beautiful, brutal coast, no longer able to withstand the battering northeast winds and the hurricane tides. Only a few will mourn her, but her essence, like that of a venerable dowager, will forever be a part of the island, even when no vestige of the structure remains. ⚓

Shortly after this piece was completed, the house and property were purchased by commercial interests. The Dowager, denied the dignity of a natural transition into obscurity, was razed.

Spangles Every Single Day

Lynne Hoffman Foster

Why did she wear spangles every single day?
Why a suit and a hat to Bible study?
To visit a sister-in-law,
to buy new sheets,
when there was nothing but sand and wind and poverty.

There were always rumblings –
"She is not like us."
Her laughter too raucous.
Her hair too brassy.
Her jewelry too shiny.
Her dinners too easy.
"No, she isn't one of us."

Then, you had two choices.
Well, three.
The church down below or the church up above.
Or neither.
That wasn't really a choice.

Mostly,
they vowed never
to marry a fisherman.
Mostly,
they did.

Paper patterns filled the drawers.
Patterns for all the dresses
she needed
for the kitchen.

Sparkling colored glass
for the ears
and the fingers
and the home-tailored suit lapel
and for next to the stretchy watch band.
It was a Timex.

There was a sort of grandeur
in the heavy red curtains
Not really velvet.
Not really grand.

It was impossible to dust.
His life covered every surface.
But then, it was her life too. ❦

Jenna Diane Willis

Jenna Diane Willis is the daughter of JoEllen and Bob Willis and is in the eighth grade at Cape Hatteras School. Her interests include theater and photography, and she hopes to become a veterinarian, possibly working with zoo animals. Her photograph "Catch of the Day" (page 31) won first place in the junior division of the 2001 Annual "Life in Hatteras" Photography Contest sponsored by the Hatteras Village Civic Association. The photo was also published in the September 2002 issue of "National Fisherman."

Hatteras, as I See It

Jenna Diane Willis

Living on Hatteras Island as a girl, I have had many advantages and opportunities that other girls living in a city wouldn't have. There is a strong sense of community, family values and safety here. I can trace my family back many generations; starting with my father and his brothers and sisters and ending with relatives who lived on Portsmouth Island in the 1700s. I have also felt safer living here than if I lived in a big city. I can walk down the road and not worry about being kidnapped or shot. I feel so safe here on this island that it doesn't scare me to sleep outside in a tent.

Besides the safety of this island, there is the pristine beauty of the ocean. I love taking long walks on the beach with my mother and just taking in everything. Between the swirls of sand on the sides of dunes and the shore birds darting at the edge of the waves searching for food, the beach is one of the most amazingly wonderful places on earth. I can go there almost anytime.

The rich tradition of Hatteras Island is just another one of the many things that sets living here apart from any other area. Traditions like "The Pirate Jamboree" and the old *Sea Chest* magazines and the current summer fish fry are traditions unique to the island. I, of course, have to mention surfing, a tradition that did not originate here but has made its home on our beaches. Although I myself do not surf, I think it really is one of the most interesting pastimes on Hatteras Island.

A tradition that my family has is collecting old bottles that we find along the sound side of the island, which came from old houses and possibly, infirmaries from the Civil War era. Although my brother and I have both found a few, it is my parents who are the real treasure hunters of the family. They have found hundreds of old bottles, some dating as far back as 1785.

There are so many great things about living on Hatteras Island that I couldn't begin to write about all of them. Even though I complain about being bored and not wanting to live here, I really do love this island and think I am blessed to be in such an amazing place. ❦

Irene Nolan

Irene Nolan, fifty-six, grew up on the East Coast as a Navy "brat." She was graduated from Indiana University with a degree in journalism and spent twenty-three years as a reporter and editor at "The Courier-Journal" in Louisville, Kentucky — the last five as managing editor. In 1989, during her tenure leading the newspaper, the staff won a Pulitzer Prize for its coverage of a church bus crash, caused by a drunken driver, that claimed the lives of twenty-seven people, mostly children. In 1991, after fifteen years of vacationing on Hatteras Island, she left the life of big-city, daily journalism, married an islander, and moved to Hatteras, where she edits "The Island Breeze," a monthly newspaper, and free-lances for other publications. Her husband died of cancer in August of 2000, but she never intends to leave Hatteras. "I have my toes firmly planted in the sand," she says. "This island is now part of me."

A Story About My Husband

Irene Nolan

This is a story about my husband, C. A. Boxley. He died on August 6. He was sixty-three years old and had been ill for three years. During those years, he had two major cancer operations, a heart attack, and quadruple bypass surgery. However, this is not an obituary.

It is a story about how his life and death on Hatteras Island has spoken to me – and to so many of his friends and family – about all that is special and unique about this place.

C. A., like so many others, loved Hatteras since the first time he saw it back in the '60s when his friend, Rob Hawkins, brought him and some other buddies from Richmond, Virginia, here to the beach to camp and fish. Over the next decade, the friends made many trips to Hatteras. They made other good friends here and many wonderful memories. By the mid '70s, C. A. was building a house on the island in Brigands' Bay. He and his friends built the house themselves – had it framed within two weeks with a lot of of hard work, long days, and many cases of Pabst Blue Ribbon, his favorite beer.

A few years later, he moved here. He was a lumber broker and was fortunate that after many years in the business, he could run it from about any place he chose with a phone, a fax, and periodic trips to visit his customers.

He ran the business from his office in his house. His desk sits in front of a window that gave him a beautiful view along the main creek into the Pamlico Sound and to the reef that parallels the island.

I knew C. A. for more than a dozen years before we were married and I moved here nine years ago. During those years he shared with me those things he loved about Hatteras. He was generous about sharing his love for this special island with all he knew – his daughters, his family, my children, my family, his business associates, and newcomers to the island.

He loved the remoteness of the island and its wild beauty. He loved the people who live here and counted among his friends both island natives and new arrivals. He admired the independence, the self-reliance, and the cleverness of the islanders. He liked sharing his skills with them – his carpentry work, for instance – and he eagerly accepted their help with such things as repairing boats and engines. One of the first lessons he taught me when I moved here was not to try to change the island or the people. Accept them as they are, he said.

He enjoyed the young people and took them hunting or told them wild stories about how he lost the tip of one finger – a shark bit it off, or he chewed his fingernails when he was a kid. He loved teaching them how to shoot or hunt or fish or find clams.

He especially loved his home and entertaining there. For many years, there was a special Memorial Day gathering for which pork shoulders roasted slowly all day on a big barbecue cooker and the beer was iced down early. He invited visitors to smaller dinners, and prepared Hatteras-style clam chowder or a really terrific Portuguese seafood stew, called cioppino.

Of course, he loved everything about the outdoor lifestyle of Hatteras.

He loved the water and the beach, touring by vehicle and by boat, clamming, crabbing, fishing and bird watching. He loved driving out to King's Point and watching the deep reds and oranges of the winter sunsets. He loved camping on the beach on Hatteras, and in recent years, we camped many times on Portsmouth Island. He enjoyed cooking dinner on the beach and all-day beach parties that included crabbing, clamming trips, and big beach fires at night.

Everyone called him the "beachmaster" – for good reasons. He knew everything there was to know about surviving an evening or a weekend on the beach – knew how to start the grill in the wind, stake down the tent so it wouldn't blow away, and make coffee in an old-fashioned percolator on a campfire. He seldom if ever forgot an essential item for a short or long trip and had been known to bring tables, cloth napkins, and wine glasses for a special dinner at the shore.

His singular passion was duck hunting. When it was cold and stormy and the wind blew hard from the northwest, he was in his element. He and his hunting buddies suited up in their coats and waders, loaded the decoys in the boat, and headed to the reef. There they hunkered down all morning in a tiny duck blind on stilts and waited for pintails to glide in over the decoys. When the hunt was over, they cooked beans over a burner on the boat and passed around a flask of apricot brandy.

He taught me how to survive a hurricane or a northeaster – how to prepare for the tide that inevitably came up in the yard and under the house, tie off the boats, and cook on the wood stove when the power went out. All of these things he shared with me, and with so many others in his lifetime.

When he became sick three years ago, I found out so much more about Hatteras. I learned how this community pulls together. Friends brought him his favorite soup when he didn't feel like eating. They looked after his boats and helped me prepare for hurricanes. They gave me emotional support when my spirits and my energy were at an all-time low. They helped me drive him to doctors off the island, and our own island physicians came to the house when he was too sick to go to the medical center. When he died last month, folks gathered around once again to support his family, affirm his life, and share their memories.

At his memorial service my son read some of the notes from his friends.

"You will never know how much you have meant to me and how much the time you spent with me changed my life in a positive way," wrote Scott Wilkinson, who as a youngster went hunting with C. A. many times. "Know that when I am hunting, a duck doesn't fly by without my thinking of you."

"It seems like C. A. has always been part of our family," wrote my niece, Angela Clare. "C. A. was the original 'beachmaster.' He helped introduce us all to the beautiful island of Hatteras – the fun, the different, the down-to-earth goodness of the people. Not a single one of us will ever again be on the beach or the deck or in the hot tub without thinking of C. A."

"I never knew any man to love his home as much as C. A.," wrote Leslie Songer, the wife of one of his business associates. "We would listen to him tell us how he could go fishing or shrimping in the morning and that very night have the freshest seafood for dinner. No storm or hurricane would drive him from his beloved home. The ocean was in his soul."

Finally, one of the notes that touched me most spoke not of his love of the island but of the man that he was. It came to me from our friend, Michal Schliff, who with her husband owned The Orange Blossom:

"When I think of C. A., I, of course, remember the tanned and robust man of a few years back – handsome, smiling, thoroughly absorbed in the richness of life. But the image of him that I carry in my heart with tenderness and respect is that of the physically frail man who seated himself carefully at our bakery table and, a spoonful at a time, doggedly consumed one bowl of our seafood chowder. It usually took about a half hour for him to eat that one bowlful of soup. I remember feeling grateful that we had the soup on the days when he came in. I grew used to seeing him, hunched determinedly over that bowl of chowder. I took those moments for granted, as if they – and he – would always go on, always be there.

"When I heard of his death, and your loss, I grieved for you – and for myself. I felt a sense of loss that I had not spent time with him when he was at our table more than to say hello, but then I realized that he had given me a great gift and that my connection with him was just as it was meant to be. The gift was in the image he burned into my heart with his slow-paced walk, his determined posture, and his dignity and humility and courage in taking sustenance. His image speaks to me now when I experience the ordinary aches and pains of living, and I am so grateful to him. I think of Peace Pilgrim's words, 'Every good thing you do vibrates on and on and never ceases.' For me, C. A. did a very good thing."

C. A. wanted to be cremated, and he wanted his remains placed in the yard of the house he loved so much. Our friend Dave Grieder, one of the island newcomers of whom C. A. was very fond, conducted a memorial service on the deck and the dock. Then we had the good, old-fashioned wake he had requested and shared our stories about him. Our friends Jamie Markley and Shelley Rollinson, sang some of his favorite songs.

C. A. did a very good thing for all of us who loved him during his lifetime, and, in death, he has made us remember all that is good and special about the place he loved so much. He was a husband, a father, a grandfather, a brother, a good friend, a teacher. We will all miss him terribly. 🐚

This first appeared in *The Island Breeze*, September 2002

Betty Swanson

Betty Swanson was born and reared in southern New Jersey. After attending a business school, she worked for several years as an executive secretary. She went on to pursue other interests, including working on an organic farm, working at island bookstores and establishing her own business as a massage therapist. Betty is currently a stay-at-home mom and assists her husband with their outdoor furniture business.

In the Name of Love

Betty Swanson

When I first moved to Hatteras Island, over thirteen years ago, I couldn't help but ask myself *What, in the name of love, have I done?* The only person I knew on the island was my fiancé, who was very busy at the time establishing his own outdoor furniture business. I was lonely and bored and homesick for family and friends and everything else that was familiar to me back home in New Jersey.

The island seemed isolated to me – as if it were somehow removed from the rest of the world. It was naturally beautiful, in a primitive way, but unlike any place else I had ever known.

To begin with, it sat thirty miles out to sea and was accessible only by ferry on the southern end or the Bonner Bridge at the northern end. There was one two-lane highway running the length of the Island, from bridge to ferry docks. I no longer had access to many of the conveniences or distractions to which I was accustomed. I now had to get used to the electricity turning off and on at random, fuzzy television reception (when the electricity was on), and preparing for floods and hurricanes. I hated living in an old trailer that was filled with holes and leaks and bugs (not to mention the mushrooms that were sprouting up through the closet floor). I especially hated the snakes that I discovered living in my own backyard. I began to wonder, was it my imagination, or did everyone on the island drive an old pickup truck with a big, black dog barking in the back? I felt I was out of my element. What initially started out as a romantic adventure had turned into something foreign and unpleasant.

While I was struggling with these feelings, my guardian angel decided to step forward and help out. She placed in my path several women who would eventually become life-long friends. Not only were these women kind and helpful, they shared with me a variety of common interests that included art, books, music, gardening and the healing arts. We also shared a passion for nature, which resulted in long walks on the beach, swimming, exploring the island on our bicycles, and hiking through the maritime woods in winter (when the snakes weren't about!). For years I had been searching for a core group of women to whom I felt connected, and here they were on Hatteras Island. Surprise, surprise.

Other avenues of interest began to open for me. By profession, I was a massage therapist and had hopes of establishing my own business when I moved to the island. Although this did not happen overnight, I gradually saw my business grow along with local interest in my work and a steady increase in tourism. It was especially gratifying, after working for a few years, to be able to hang my own shingle outside my office – Betty Swanson, Certified Massage Therapist – rather than continue carrying my massage table, and all the paraphernalia it entailed, up and down two or three flights of stairs in order to give at-home massages. For me, having my own office was a big step in adding a sense of professionalism to my work.

I also decided to take advantage of some of the activities and continuing education courses offered by various island facilities. I enrolled in a beginner's computer course, learned how to knit with a group of women who met weekly at the local bookstore, and wrote my first haiku at a creative writing workshop. Since volunteer work was a large part of island life, I signed up at the elementary school to help children with their math and English assignments. Participating in bake sales, church activities and fund raisers became new experiences for me that were fun and rewarding.

Eventually, the "Island Life" began to work its magic on me. I grew to cherish the closeness and familiarity that came with living in a small community. The diversity of the people, combined with their resilience and resourcefulness (especially after a hurricane), was refreshing. The isolation of place and lack of familiar distractions were actually a gift that forced me to get to know myself better. I felt grateful to my fiancé, who was now my husband, for introducing me to the island in spite of my original misgivings. I was particularly grateful that he and I were rearing our daughter together in this unique place we now called home.

People and places may not always be what they seem at first glance. It takes time to get to know a place. It takes time to get to know people. Most important, it takes time, and patience, to get to know yourself and to find the place where you really belong. 🌴

Haiku

Betty Swanson

Seagulls dive and swoop
Begging for scattered breadcrumbs
Beyond the boat's wake.

Soft incoming surf
Marriage of sand and water
Seashells left behind.

Busy buzzing bees
Pollen stuck to spindly legs
Pansies in full bloom. 🌾

Yes, Even Here

Our book is a collection exploring all the things that are special about or unique to Hatteras Island from the perspectives of its women. When we solicited submissions, the response was an enthusiastic celebration of thought and creativity. One woman came forward requesting a piece about domestic violence, which occurs everywhere in the world, and is certainly not unique to Hatteras Island. Her thought was that even here in what some perceive to be paradise, reality can be stark and painful, and domestic abuse happened to her. Her voice said that although she suffered as a victim, she celebrated her survival. She chose for various reasons not to write of her own experience.

I followed up on her request, sought more information, and spoke with others involved with the issue of domestic violence on Hatteras Island. Lynn Bryant, executive director of Outer Banks Hotline, was an invaluable source of statistics and commentary. "The Voices of Hatteras Island Women" must include the truth of hardship as well as happiness. I chose to write the following for those reasons, and because it happened to me.

Linda Elizabeth Nunn

Perspectives on Domestic Violence

Linda Elizabeth Nunn

For many, living on Hatteras Island offers the sort of life befitting a modern pioneer, although the relative isolation of this remote haven can take its toll on relationships. Tightly knit families and communities reticent about opening to outside resources may contribute to the isolation felt by a woman in an abusive relationship. Drug abuse and alcoholism, more widely spread on the island than is initially apparent, contribute to the problem. Lack of on-site opportunity for education beyond high school, and economic hardship also play a role in hindering the woman seeking relief from an abusive situation. Attitudes of shame, guilt and ignorance, or "It's not my problem," or even "What problem?" do nothing to relieve the situation.

From a survivor: "I was sitting in a women's circle meeting at church and was not looking forward to the topic, domestic violence. As we read the various parts of the service, we saw the awful consequences of domestic violence on a national level. We heard of women and children suffering terribly. Inwardly, I cringed. I did not want to re-open these wounds. 'I must stay calm. I can do this,' became my mantra. I was doing really well until the discussion part when one of the women spoke up.

"'Isn't it great that we don't have that problem on the island?' she asked.

"I never heard the other responses. I felt like I was going to throw up, and rushed out of the room. I retreated to a quiet place and was consoled by my closest friend and the pastor's wife, who knew of my circumstances. As tears poured down my face, I fought an overwhelming urge to shriek at that woman *Are you blind? Can you not see the pain around you?*"

According to Outer Banks Hotline's 2002 statistical reports, 416 women in Dare County sought information and referral for situations that were mentally, emotionally, financially and/or physically abusive. Ninety-three women sought shelter in the Battered Women's Shelter in Manteo, and about 25 percent of those women came from Hatteras Island. That number has even more significance in view of the 2000 census figures from the Outer Banks Chamber of Commerce: Hatteras Island residents accounted for only 13 percent of Dare County's total population. Lynn Bryant, Hotline's executive director, says that the number of women from Hatteras Island seeking shelter may have been higher if the women involved had not also faced the additional challenges of getting to work and keeping their children in school.

The first woman who sought help at the shelter when it opened in 1994 was from Hatteras Island. She literally sat in her car and waited while someone made up her bed. Another survivor offers: "For me, the worst abuse was not physical. Sure, I had a broken nose, was regularly black and blue with bruises, and had even been hospitalized. The worst was the verbal abuse. The constant negative phrases, the tearing away at my soul: he was always telling me I was worthless, and that no one would want me after he was through with me. I began to believe the lies. I became 'brainwashed.' That's why it was so hard to leave."

Taking the first step in getting out of an abusive relationship means acknowledging the problem and asking for help. It means relying on courage many women do not believe they possess.

"When I walked out that door, I left everything," another survivor adds. "I knew my life depended on it. How could someone who loved me become so consumed with hate and anger?"

No matter the excuses or reasons, whether an abusive situation escalates because of economic hardship, drug abuse, emotional frustration, instability, or a combination of factors, the abuser's irresponsibility brings him into a system – either through counseling and/or legal involvement.

"People often come to court-appointed anger management sessions full of resentment," explains one counselor. "They cannot understand why they are being prosecuted. They really don't think they have done anything wrong."

Abusers offer their explanations: "These things wouldn't happen if she would just straighten up. I mean, she can't do nothing right. Can't cook the way I like, can't iron my shirts right, says she is tired when she gets home from work, can't keep the kids quiet. I thought about getting rid of her, but then I'd just have to train someone else." And: "When we argue, things really get out of control. We get louder and louder and say mean things to each other. Then I get really burned up and want to hit something. I really try not to hit her. I've busted holes in the walls and thrown stuff. I just can't stop being angry. When it is over and I look at her, I can't believe what I've done. Hell, I can't even remember what I've done. God, I'm sorry. I'm really so damn sorry."

Women on Hatteras Island seeking relief from domestic violence receive counseling and necessarily become involved with the legal system. Although Hotline members and law enforcement personnel work hard to provide protection and offer resolution to the situations, survivors of domestic abuse may have less than positive encounters. Survivors report: "Why does there have to be this 'good ol' boys' network? My husband was put in jail when he violated the 50B protective order. And the judge had him out before I could even leave the island!" Another woman says: "I was at my attorney's office, waiting to get a court order to protect me from my estranged husband. I carried pepper spray and my apartment doors had new locks on them. My attorney turned on the speakerphone and I heard someone say, 'Today's not a good day to try and get that order. The judge said he is tired of all these women coming in for protection when they have a little tiff with their husbands. The next one will have to come in dragging and bleeding before I'll issue another order.'"

Yes, Hatteras Island offers a unique lifestyle to its women. We learn to live in tandem with nature, with the sea, going about our daily chores and pleasures with that special feeling of living out here "on the edge." We take pride in the island heritage, and we grow concerned with the changes coming on perhaps too fast. We acknowledge that our lifestyle here makes us different from women living in other areas of the country – and of the world – yet we also know that our basic commonality unites us with women everywhere. Domestic violence exists on Hatteras Island as it does elsewhere, and we can work toward increased public awareness, toward resolutions of all the issues contributing to the problem, toward a time when no woman will have to stand up and tell a story like this:

"The fourth time I ended up in the emergency room, I knew I couldn't keep on like that. I lay in the cubicle, my right arm in a cast, an ice pack on my left eye, fuzzy from the pain medication, and wondered how I would care for my kids, do laundry, make meals, go to work, with a broken arm. I tried to think of a story to tell the neighbors, my folks. A nurse came in, put a glass of juice on the table and said, 'You know, you don't have to do this anymore.' She placed a slip of paper with a phone number on it in my hand, and left quietly. Maybe it was because of courage, but more likely desperation, I called that number the next day, and began a new life." ☕

Marcia Lyons

After earning a degree in wildlife biology, Marcia Lyons moved to Hatteras Island in 1976. With a long-term interest in coastal systems, Marcia has worked for the National Park Service as a naturalist, an educator, and more recently as a field biologist. She married and reared a son here, and says that the ocean lured her to this place nearly thirty years ago. "The wild, remote islands that I found back then have kept me from leaving," she says.

This article was adapted from a bulletin circulated by the National Park Service. As a biologist with a keen interest in coastal ecology, Marcia Lyons chose to contribute the information as her participation in this anthology.

From Turtles to Birds, Visitors Need to Help Protect Wildlife at Cape Hatteras National Seashore

Marcia Lyons

The Cape Hatteras National Seashore is home for coastal wildlife, including nesting, threatened and endangered sea turtles, and numerous birds, including the threatened piping plover. It is essential for persons coming to the National Seashore to remember they are not the only visitors to the beaches. Finding a balance between human activity and protecting native wildlife can be difficult at times, but there are many ways visitors can help reach this balance.

Sea turtles are known to have been caught and entangled in items left on the beach. Tent-like shade structures, beach furniture and volleyball nets with anchor ties present a danger to these giant reptiles. At one point, ten shade structures were found left on the beach near Frisco. At the end of the day, visitors must remove their belongings from National Park Service beaches, which include beaches adjacent to all Hatteras Island villages.

One of the rights of passage for children when they visit the beach is to dig holes and build sandcastles in the sand. Unfortunately, large, deep holes left on the beach can be a danger not only to the unwary sea turtle crawling ashore to nest, but also to individuals walking the beach, especially at night. Families should enjoy digging these "holes to China," but for the safety of both humans and sea turtles, they should be filled in before leaving the beach.

The high tide can not be counted on to fill in most of these cavernous holes.

Artificial lighting can keep adult sea turtles from nesting. Emerging hatchlings can be disoriented as they attempt to steer toward the natural light reflection from the ocean. Streetlights, buildings, fishing piers, off-road vehicles and campfires are some of the sources emitting artificial light. Those residing in beach cottages can help by turning off unneeded outside lights and shading indoor lights. Campfires (not bonfires) are permitted in the seashore if placed below the high tide line. They should never be built near a posted turtle nest site. Trash, beer cans and bottles should not be burned in the fires. Glass bottles break in the fire and could cut someone's foot or a sea turtle's flipper.

If visitors driving an off-road vehicle happen upon a nesting turtle, they should turn their lights away and leave the area so as not to disturb the nesting activity. The same follows true for people walking down the beach with flashlights. Such disturbances can cause a female turtle to abort her nesting attempt.

All known sea turtle nest sites are posted for their protection. As hatching dates approach, closures must be enlarged to safeguard the young. Beachgoers should respect these signed areas at all times. Areas are re-opened after hatching is completed.

Beach bird-nesting sites are seasonally closed to the public along the National Seashore as well. Entry into these closed areas could cause nesting adults to abandon nests, allowing eggs and chicks to succumb to the heat. Entry could also cause injury when protective terns dive-bomb intruders. Persons should also refrain from flying kites over these bird closures. Kites can resemble predators and quickly agitate birds. Many of these closures are at the ends of the islands and are subject to occasional high tides. Persons planning outings in these areas especially near times of extreme high tide should check tide charts so they will not be trapped between the tide and a bird closure. Trash attracts predators, so leaving the beach clean is important. In all National Park Service sites it is illegal to feed any wildlife.

Dogs are allowed in the seashore if leashed at all times. Pets attracted to nesting sites can seriously harm eggs and chicks. They also chase migrating shorebirds that need resting and feeding time before continuing their long flights, often across open ocean.

Fireworks are not allowed in any parts of the seashore, including the ocean beaches. In addition to being a safety concern, their luminous lights and loud noises can disrupt nesting birds and turtles.

Cape Hatteras National Seashore was established for the enjoyment of the people as well as for the protection and preservation of the islands' natural resources. Visitors flock here for recreational opportunities as well as to enjoy the coastal beauty and its wildlife. Visitors are encouraged to follow simple guidelines to help ensure that these natural resources are saved for future generations.

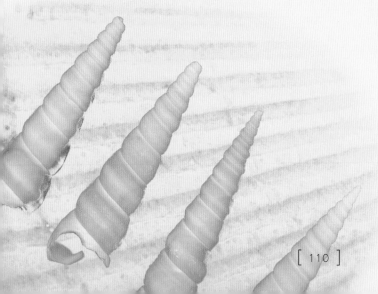

ILLUSTRATION AND PHOTO CREDITS

Reader Response

We would appreciate any comments you may have about *A Hatteras Anthology*, and welcome inquiries regarding author appearances and book signings.

Please mail your response to Outer Banks Press, Post Office Box 2829, Kitty Hawk, NC 27949, Attn: Hatteras Anthology. You may also fax your reply to (252) 261-0613 or send an e-mail to anthology@outerbankspress.com.